17.25

D0206450

In *The Company of Strangers*

In
THE COMPANY
OF STRANGERS

MARY MEIGS

TALONBOOKS 1991

PENTICTON PUBLIC LIBRARY

Copyright © 1991 Mary Meigs

Published with the assistance of the Canada Council

Talonbooks
201 / 1019 East Cordova
Vancouver
British Columbia V6A 1M8
Canada

Designed by Stephen Osborne
Black-and-white internegs prepared by Ann Pearson
Photographs: Alison Burns—pages 39, 49, 73, 80, 109, 134, 145, 154;
    Gloria Demers—pages 65, 93, 126 and back cover; Ron S.
    Diamond—pages 2, 11, 59, 118, 149
Typeset in Stempel Garamond and Futura by The Vancouver Desktop
    Publishing Centre Ltd.
Printed and bound in Canada by Hignell Printing Ltd.

Fourth printing: July 1993

Canadian Cataloguing in Publication Data
Meigs, Mary, 1917-
    In the company of strangers

    ISBN 0-99822-294-0

    1. Company of strangers (Motion picture)
I. Title.
PN1997.C65M4 1991   791.43'72   C91-091442-7

CONTENTS

I should like to dedicate this book to the seven other members of the cast: Alice, Beth, Catherine, Cissy, Constance, Michelle, Winnie. To Cynthia and Sally, and to the memory of Gloria, who died July 19, 1989, without having seen the finished film, and to all the other makers of *The Company of Strangers*.

With thanks to Carole Robertson, who with superhuman patience typed and retyped my manuscript on her computer. To Pauline Delaronde, who wrote out words and sentences in the Mohawk language and translated them for the chapter "Tekahawákwen (Alice)." And to Mary Schendlinger, my eagle-eyed longtime editor and friend.

The gramophone was affirming in tones there was no denying, triumphant yet valedictory: *Dispersed are we, who have come together. But, the gramophone asserted, let us retain whatever made that harmony.*

—VIRGINIA WOOLF, *BETWEEN THE ACTS*

PREFACE

"Who are these women? Why are they together? Where are they going?" The answers to these questions lie not in *The Company of Strangers,* but in Gloria Demers' scenarios, dated April 28 and June 15, 1988. They state that what Gloria called "our eclectic group of seniors" is being taken in a rented school bus (the working title of the film was *The Bus*) "to a Golden Age exchange program at some remote resort." We are "eclectic" because we come from different backgrounds and don't know each other. Seven of us are over 65; the eighth, who drives our bus, is Michelle Sweeney, 27, in real life a gospel and jazz singer. We are all "in real life," since we are ourselves in a semi-documentary, or "alternative drama." Our semi or alternative category shapes our story, which has no plot and no conventional drama; it is a happening in which strangers become company. The bus "runs gently off the road into a ditch," says Gloria, as we make a detour to find Constance Garneau's childhood house. The bus dies twice, once at the beginning and once in the middle of the film and both of its deaths are essential to our leisurely evolution as friends; we need an imprecise amount of time to improvise practical solutions and to get to know each other through tête-à-tête conversations. The solutions were retained from the scenario but most of Gloria's dialogue was shed and we were allowed to arrive at a scene's objective in our own way.

During the filming, which spanned the summer of 1988, none of us knew what the film was about or why we made up "the eclectic group." We could only have answered the first of the questions that people ask: who are these women? We knew who we were; we were ourselves, who, we did not quite know why, had been judged suitable to be in the cast. *The Company of Strangers* was written, it says in the final scenario, by "Gloria Demers, with Cynthia Scott, David Wilson, and Sally Bochner." Each of these had other titles: Cynthia was Director; Gloria was also Associate Director; Sally was Associate Producer; David Wilson was both Producer and Editor. The filmmakers' work is hidden from us (the cast) in a mist that resembles the mist from which we emerge at the beginning of the film. To me, the mist symbolizes the absence of explanation. The audience is asked to believe that none is needed; the mist cuts us off from reasons, and lifts to show us, who have stepped out of time and logic into a magic space where old women have room to exist. We are, at the time of filming: Alice Diabo, 74; Constance Garneau, 88; Winifred Holden, 76; Cissy Meddings, 76; Mary Meigs, 71; Catherine Roche, 65; Beth Webber, 80.

POSTPREAMBLE

October 6, 1990. *The Company of Strangers* is aloft. It climbs on the updraughts, and floats like a planing bird over seas and continents without bothering to beat its wings. All of us who shared in the making of the film are in a happy daze, for we could not guess, only hope in the secret places of our day-dreams, that it would have this future. The members of the cast, the eight of us who were strangers to each other and became company during the summer of 1988, exchange our incredulous amazement. Some of the cast fly with the film from city to city, ride to premières in stretch limousines, are fêted at gala parties, are interviewed and appear on television. They come back with memorabilia: menus, shower caps and soap from their hotel rooms, which they bestow on the stay-at-homes. Alice, Beth, Winnie, who relish excitement and appear to be tireless, appear with Cynthia on the TV screen with other-worldly, beaming

11

expressions. They have been touched with a magic wand. The interviewers beam, too, for the special power of our film is to make people happy.

Constance and I stay home and share tidbits on the telephone: heartwarming reviews, letters from friends who have seen the film, a first prize which Cynthia receives at Mannheim, news of an award from the Halifax film festival for the group of eight, for "best actresses." "It should have been 'best semi-actresses'," I say to Beth. Beth has longed all her life (she is 82 now) to be a real actress, but no success she has ever imagined can compare to the splendour of this one. She wants it to go on forever; she will fly to New York, to London, anywhere the film flies. "Who could possibly have thought this would happen . . . ?" her voice trails off in speechless wonder. Winnie says, "I can't stand a lot of adulation. Do you like it?" I say that I would never have survived, that interviews scare me, that big parties bring on fits of shyness. This is ninety-five per cent of the truth. The rest is hidden in the shadow of Gloria's death over a year ago, before she saw the finished film. I was in the film because Gloria wanted an affirmation of lesbian existence, because she stood by me when I gave it.

Cynthia and David Wilson must have felt Gloria's presence in the cutting-room after she died, willing the film to move according to her dream. The finished film is a loving homage to Gloria from Cynthia and all the others; we all think of Gloria's joy that should have been. She would have delighted in the standing ovations, the parties and flights from triumph to triumph. Gloria is invisibly there, and her scenario still remains as the invisible scaffolding of the film. As it turned out, our improvised dialogue gave the film a shape that corresponded strangely to Cynthia's and Gloria's dream. We seven old women and a younger woman were bound into a landscape and bound to each other in the course of making the film. The landscape was not the backdrop for a semi-documentary; it was a multiple metaphor for old age, memory, life and death. We became company with each other and with our landscape. Gloria would have said to Cynthia, "This is what we dreamed of," and she would have flashed me a v-shaped smile.

What follows is my story of how it happened.

SUI GENERIS

My doorbell rings (January 12, 1988); I open the door to two women, unfamiliar to me, and realize that they must be from the National Film Board, friends of a friend. They are scouting around for old women ("older," said my friend tactfully) to be in a semi-documentary film. Looking at them, I have no presentiment that they have entered the space of my life and will give it a new shape. One of the two has long blond hair, a face like a Valkyrie, blue eyes that are accustomed to looking, appraising. Absently today, as though it is neither here nor there, as though her purpose in coming is to be determined by what she sees (these are ex-post-facto thoughts). She is Cynthia Scott, who will direct the film. The other woman is Gloria Demers, amply curvy with a straight, flat back; she has brown eyes and a friendly face. She looks like Cathy in the comic strip. "I *am* Cathy," she says much later, and eventually Gloria and

Cathy merge for me, with their deliberately goofy smiles and rolling eyes and fits of guilt and unpredictable rage. Gloria is wearing a brown Irish sweater, rumpled corduroy pants and running shoes, Cynthia a jumpsuit and running shoes. I show them the house from top to bottom; I babble; I think (incorrectly) that they are lovers.

They are sizing me up in the course of our aimless talk. Cynthia's mind is operating like a camera lens; what she says is absentminded, or imprecise; she needs images. Her vocabulary lies in images beyond my vision that will take human shape. She already has an idea of who will fit, how and why. No, not *how*, for there is no scenario (Gloria will write it). Not that I know any of this; I know nothing about how films are made. I have no sense of being on trial, for I don't take any of it seriously. These two friendly people have come and are uttering sounds of delight about my house. Even though I've assumed that they are lovers, it takes a long time before any of us pronounces the word "lesbian." "The L-word," says Gloria with a sigh of relief, rolling her eyes à la Cathy. Even at this point, I don't feel the net being drawn in. The L-word has been introduced into the conversation and has attached itself to me in a nonviolent way. Cynthia gives no sign of caring, no sighs of relief from her. Something decidedly non-lesbian about this, I see in retrospect. Lesbians look for clues. Clothes? Ease with women? Some women are wonderfully at ease with us because they know that we will have the sense not to cross the invisible line, like a strung wire that will shear off our heads if we speak the word. We have sixth senses for spotting the imperceptible stiffening; we can read the questions in women's heads: "Shall I speak now of my husband, lover, ex-lover, children?" Just as a man artlessly lets fall the words, "My wife" (even with me). On this particular day, however, my intuition is fogged by the evidence of two women casually dressed, and with a common purpose that I can't fathom, for the subject of the film seems so vast: the whole spectrum of old ("older") women in Montreal, and it will only be by gathering hundreds of old women, sifting through them painstakingly, that a pattern can be seen. Cynthia and Gloria and the other decision-makers will know the subject after all these interviews and try-outs. Certain women will contain the subject. Or will the subject (scenario) be running along on another track? Will the women act or be themselves? It doesn't occur to me that Cynthia and Gloria have begun the process of fitting me into an image—hypothetical—of someone as yet unknown to them. Now I conjecture that each had images swarming in her head and every now and then a flesh-and-blood woman, one of us who ended up in the cast, would fall into the swarm and merge with the pattern-image. This process of *knowing* whether we will fit takes a long time, particularly since they do not necessarily always agree; it is the time when we are in limbo, without the least idea of their criteria.

Gloria, though, has a relatively simple image; she is looking for a lesbian. As it happens, I don't at all fit the person she expected me to be. "I think my image was of a short, wire-spectacled, plump, dress-wearing, 'passing for straight,' Westmount matron," she says in a letter, April 19, 1989. "I must have grinned when I saw the real you—so tall, so very slim, so much white hair, big glasses. Reeboks on your feet!" I think the Westmount matron was one of those discouraging images the subconscious invents in order to induce a pleasant surprise. Or was she a stock film-version of a lesbian, who looks like Everywoman, about whom women in the audience will say, "But she's just like us!" She is "passing for straight," she deflects the stereotype. The new vision, the woman with white hair, wearing Reeboks, struck Gloria like the lightning bolt that hit Paul on the road to Damascus. It changed her life, the year and a half she had left to live, and twined her life and death inextricably with mine. In her mind she wrote a best-case scenario. I would be in the film, "for all your sisters," she says in her letter. "You had to do it again: come out for the team and lead the corps, please to show the world that this beautiful, talented, erudite woman was one of the unspeakable ten percent." (What team? What corps? I thought later, glad that they had been nonexistent.) Her best case was the imperative, desperate wish of a person who longed for happiness all her life and now sees it within reach. Some of it came true: I agreed to be in the film; I tell Cissy in our bird-watching scene that I'm a lesbian; Gloria and I became friends. And then a worst-case scenario, the fatal shadow on Gloria's lung, turned the best case into a nightmare.

On the day of the visit, the coming out of the L-word brings relief, along with a sudden wariness, for there it is like a teleprompt, "You are the lesbian I want for the film." But I think, no, to being a token lesbian; no, too, to acting the part of a lesbian. I lean in spirit toward Cynthia, who seems not to care, who seems to realize without saying it that lesbians wriggle uneasily when the word is thrown over us, obliterating everything about us except *that*. According to Gloria, we talked about it. "What was said after that? Your saying that you were not *only* a lesbian? Cyn saying she didn't want your lesbian self? My interrupting and saying that is *so* part of the self we wanted?" So from the very beginning, the two halves of me, courageous and fearful, are represented by Gloria and Cynthia. If I had looked into a crystal ball I would have seen Cynthia's view prevailing, would have seen how deftly she dealt with the idea "not *only* a lesbian," would have felt my own relief. "Did we argue right there in front of you?" Gloria goes on. "I remember leaving and not feeling too positive about your ever consenting to be in the film, but I was desperate for it to happen—as much for me as for the film. I wanted to know you better and had nothing of interest to offer you except *The Bus* [the working title]. I would do my utmost to get you to accept the role of yourself."

But on this day in January I have no sense that I am already one of those who are caught in the invisible drift-net that is being drawn tighter with every acquiescent movement I make, every little frolic in this strange new experience. Will I come to the Film Board, do some try-outs? Well, why not? There are hundreds of us in the drift-net, though we don't know it, for we come in little groups. Some of us are gently tipped out of the net; some of us perform like dolphins. It is fun, but of course it isn't serious, I think, as the net tightens. I begin to have a sense of alarm, however, when it becomes clear that I'm the lesbian who fits the image in Gloria's head, though not necessarily in Cynthia's. Cynthia is trying out the idea, why do we need a lesbian? Is it Gloria's condition for working on the film? Is the cast chosen according to categories? Is it pure chance that in the end it is composed of three Englishwomen, a black woman, a Mohawk woman, a Roman Catholic nun, a lesbian, a French-Canadian of American birth? Certainly the directors did not set out to choose three of any category, and the English trio (all long-term Canadian citizens) was pure coincidence. We were all conspicuously different one from the other, and perhaps the criterion can be deduced from that, that each of us was to be sui generis?

Back then, I was ignorant of the whole universe of filmmaking, knew almost nothing about the huge double organism, the National Film Board and l'Office National du Film, sprawled out beside the roar of the Metropolitan Boulevard, a single building divided by an intangible language wall, through which pass bilingual film people, but which to a large extent screens out knowledge by one side of what the other is doing. Ten years ago I had been hurried through the maze of corridors to see an ONF showing of *La Toile d'Araignée*, a film about Québec artists (including me) made by Jacques Giraldeau. This time I am in the anglophone sector and the language of the film will be English. Later, Constance and I murmur conspiratorially about this, its political implications, etc.; we long for an intermingling in the film of the two solitudes, but are satisfied with the explanation that the decision is based on questions of budget and subtitles.

The sizing-up period goes on for weeks, with Cynthia,

Gloria, Sally there at the Film Board day after day, with a cameraman, a sound-person, and hundreds of women from every part of Montreal where anglophones abound. Cynthia, Sally, Gloria are the fisherwomen and we are the fish, and like fish, some of us put up a fight. We are scared of the unknown, of the disruption of our lives; we thrash and try to leap over the net while we are hauled slowly in. Some of the hundreds, who have seen the ad in *The Gazette*, who have flocked to the Film Board and who long to be in the film, are, paradoxically, released from the net. The recalcitrant ones have to be played, or rather wooed, each in the same way (we compare notes later), with moral pressure, flattery and even tears, while we continue to gasp feebly that we have other plans for the summer. The technique of persuasion is so skillful that I, at least, get the impression that the entire schedule can be rearranged to accommodate my plans for the summer; the hours, the days, can be reduced (though a rather ominous number of days—thirty—remain to be squeezed in somewhere).

Is it believable that we were glad when another two weeks were added on after the thirty-day period? Proof of how we became willing slaves who were going to weep buckets of tears when the end finally came. But before it even starts, I say, "I'm afraid of being exhausted." I know this, at least, have been told by all the friends who feed me information about the rigours of filmmaking. I quote them, thinking to shore up my case. "I hate your friends," cries Gloria. "Of course we'll have a doctor on the set," says Sally, "we've thought of that possibility." The idea of a doctor, on the alert for "that possibility" stirs up new alarm in me. As it happens, there is no doctor on the set, but a retired directress of nursing, Edna Lee, who dances and sings and tells stories and spends endless hours of sitting, with an inner alarm system tuned to the slightest wobble among us, signs of over-exertion, a rise in blood pressure. I think it is Edna's presence that exerts such a strong spell against real disaster. But my forebodings are correct; I am exhausted. "What exhausts you?"

asks Constance (88 then), when I complain to her at the end of a long day. Constance only occasionally admits to being "a little tired." I am surprised again and again by the general stoicism, or is it a secret store of energy that gets the others through days that sometimes go on for fourteen hours? I hatch a theory: that this secret store is the residue of long hours of mother-work, waiting, watching, lifting, rushing around, never having enough sleep. And in the case of the nonmothers (Winnie, Catherine), training by jobs or duties, merciless schedules imposed by others. My kind of artist's discipline, which seems rigorous to me, hasn't prepared me for the hours and the use of time so unlike my own.

At the Film Board try-outs we are paired off in little scenes: one of us is huddled in misery, her husband has left her for another woman—but she stops in the middle like a balky horse; he would never do such a thing, she objects. In another scene I work myself into a fury at a taxi driver because (I say) he is contemptuous of old women with white hair; I complain that no one is interested in old women; I give a little lecture on ageism. In other scenes I am an artist, and these are easy; I can only feel comfortable when I am "playing" myself. Cynthia, Sally, Gloria are in the process of composing with us, live women, moving us around to see where we are real, where false. Our insistence on being ourselves is one of the elements of Cynthia's composition. To find what is true by making us play untruth to ourselves? I do a scene with Cissy (the only one of the cast whom I met then): we are in her garden; I'm sitting on a stool with my sketchbook. Cissy is a very small woman who looks like Mrs. Tiggy-Winkle, all bundled up, with a woollen cap pulled down to her eyebrows. "Do you mind if I draw you?" "Ow now," she says. She is planting imaginary chives in her imaginary garden, shakes in the seeds, pats the earth, then straightens up to tell me how they look when they come up, how the stem comes up crooked (she crooks her finger). We both like playing this scene of ourselves. It begins to be clear to me that naturalness is one of the virtues that Cynthia, Sally, Gloria are seeking and will find in each of us. Later, on the real set, a scene will be false, will have to be repeated the instant one of us "acts." So and so will go a little "over the top." She is over-acting, in other words. We aren't even sure of how our "real" selves are perceived; isn't a state of being over the top sometimes the temptation of a real self? It is the temptation to embellish our simple scenario, to put some creative fire into it. For an audience isn't likely to say, "How well you did that scene," when one has simply been oneself. It is hard to get into all our heads that "acting" is a sin and that it won't do us a bit of good. We're not told, however, that these fugitive moments of really throwing ourselves into a "role" will probably be cut. Perhaps they will be the easiest parts to cut, the ones about which everyone agrees?

It took months to choose, from January until June, months of our combined uncertainties and backsliding, of our not knowing, since we did not know each other, that the choice of us eight women would bind us into an entity, that the particles of our lives would open up and make room for our shared particles, and we would no longer be ourselves, the same old selves. At that time some of us were like apparently docile animals that suddenly refuse to be rounded up, and gallop off in a panic—a terrible time for the directors, who had by then determined what they wanted so precisely that each of our attempts to escape was seen as a catastrophe.

I began to suffer the instant after I had mailed a letter that put a final no in writing. I had signed a death warrant, a refusal to live a new experience. Now, three years later, I have blurred memories of stewing in my regrets, of calling the Film Board to say I'd changed my mind, of an ominous silence and then more try-outs. Cynthia and Gloria had saved me from my nay-saying self and were leading me toward the new one, who had the good sense even then to be deeply grateful to them.

THE CHÂTEAU
BORGHESE .

June 22, 1988: At the Château Borghese. My room is face to face
with a low wooded mountain, up which climb scrubby aspens,
cedars, pines. Last night after a seemingly endless drive from
Montreal in the red NFB van, which tipped us into a ditch today,
we came out on the superhighway at St. Jovite and turned back
on a road that leads to the Château Borghese, sitting high up
like a stranded white cruise ship. It is visible from the highway,
which has sliced in two the landscape around St. Jovite and
spoiled its serene beauty forever. Trailer trucks roar westward
and eastward, cars are ejected, full of summer tourists en route
to the village. There they will eat in one of the many old houses
à la Marc-Elie Fortin that have been turned into restaurants or
boutiques, perhaps in one with pink tablecloths, pink napkins,
a smiling pink-cheeked woman wearing a pink frilly apron. Or
they will go to play tennis in a monstrously inflated Something

(certainly not a building) that we called the Queen Bee, opposite the Château Borghese, pale and puffy with segments that seemed to ripple ominously in the wind. St. Jovite, like other villages painters once loved, has become a tourist paradise, with something for every taste, from fish'n'chips to Chateaubriand with sauce Béarnaise. And for us, too, the most exciting escapade imaginable after a hard day's work would be to cross the highway, peer into shop windows and sit at a table with a pink tablecloth.

The Château Borghese is an architectural melting pot: brown timbers and white stucco over cement blocks, a classy ski lodge designed for couples with muscular legs to carry them up the double flight of sharp stone steps to the front door and the steel stairs inside, thinly carpeted and hollow-sounding. If people over sixty had been consulted they would have stated the need for an elevator, non-hazardous bathtubs, lampshades that let in some light, windows that could be made to stay open, etc. etc. They would have approved, though, of the dining room, which gives an authentic impression of dazzle and luxury, with blue and white flowered linen tablecloths, tall stemmed glasses and elaborate silverware, all winking in the morning sun or the evening candlelight. At mealtimes we sat at our long table and gazed out at the highway humming with trucks, at the Queen Bee, at clouds building over the mountains behind St. Jovite. Every evening we surveyed the menu, printed in French and Italian, which was incomprehensible to five out of eight of us and had to be translated into the queen's English. Some of us had no use for Potage Crècy or la Crème Andalouse or Vitello Limone, and preferred plain hamburger or a poached egg, and Salada tea rather than any of the eight kinds of tisane, which provoked disdainful sniffs. Properly made tea was necessary to Cissy's British soul, and if it was served in the form of a pot of hot water with an inert teabag lying beside it, she sent it back to the kitchen to be steeped. She was also allergic to melon and turned pale at the sight of sliced cantaloupe, screwing up her face as if a plate of live scorpions had been set in front of her. Alice hated rice and liked potatoes; Constance ordered rashly and was almost always depressed by the first bite. She got to her feet, having left her plate untouched, and wandered over to contemplate the chocolate layer cake and pastries on a side table, and came back looking like a guilty schoolgirl. Later I discovered that Constance and Gloria shared a passion for chocolates and cakes (only the best, of course) and could linger in front of the window of Andrée's with an expression of bliss and longing on their faces.

The Château Borghese is run by Angelo and his companion Margaret. Angelo had been employed as maître d'h at the great hotels of Europe, he told us, and has photographs of himself in the company of crowned heads and other worthies to prove it. He has a melancholy, long-nosed face and has learned the detached airs of the perfect maître d'h; as manager he manages limply, distractedly, with an air of having onerous duties elsewhere. He welcomes, he makes drinks, he makes trips to Montreal, he brings exotic fish from Waldman's, which appears at dinner as tilefish à la sauce de fenouil. In matters of haute cuisine, Angelo considered us sadly ignorant, for why did we complain about the tilefish or keep sending the vegetables, raw à la mode, back to the microwave? When Angelo set down his vongole in front of Michelle, she looked at it coolly and said, "You got any of that Parmesan cheese, or maybe some meat sauce?" Angelo groaned. "Put meat sauce on my 500-year-old recipe!" He brought a bowl of grated cheese and Michelle dumped it over her vongole. "It really needs some meat sauce," she said. "We don't have any meat sauce. We don't have *any* sauce!" cried Angelo. His sensibilities of grand chef were bruised over and over again by every one of us.

Margaret, Angelo's wife, is a slender, delicate-looking Québecoise with a cloud of dark, curly hair, who had gone to the same private school in Montreal as Gloria. She showed us a photograph and only the sharpest of us (Winnie) recognized either of them in the crowd of very young schoolgirls, whose faces gave no hint of their future. The poetic and romantic in Margaret must have been drawn to Angelo, his hard childhood and subsequent glory as a maître d'h. For me, he was a mystery full of Italian charm, mock (or real) despair, histrionics, sinuous sexiness and thoughtfulness. Signs of the latter materialized every day; the schedule of the Château Borghese was turned upside down to suit our hours, early rising and late wandering back for dinner, our sometimes crotchety tastes. Some of us were used to a simpler style of life and secretly wished to trade places with the crew members who had been billeted at the Rivière Rouge, on a bank of a river of the same name, frequented by types who did not dress for dinner.

The Château Borghese was part of the magic realm we entered when we left Montreal. Even under its spell, though, there were intimations of mortality: Beth's falls and almost-falls downstairs, her sprained ankle, Constance's lurid bruises and high blood pressure, followed by a precipitous trip to the clinic in St. Jovite. Edna held periodic blood-pressure seances in the television room, to detect the effects of too much stress or too much excitement, but real accidents did not prevent the victims from playing their scenes on schedule. Beth walked warily on her strapped-up ankle; Constance's face was the colour of a rainbow, and she had an angry wound on her arm, but we would not be permitted either in real life or in the final scenario, to be seriously disabled or to die. Maybe our blind faith in magic made us foolhardy. Beth sometimes seemed to throw herself headlong down steps as though she could fly; at the Rivière Rouge she sped heedlessly across the dining room like a duck running on water before takeoff, and landed spread-eagled on the dance platform, her senses in a daze. We all pushed ourselves beyond our known limits, propelled by the same faith with which Catherine (in the film) set out on her arthritic feet (real) for a thirty-kilometre walk and greeted us the next day from the pontoon of a seaplane.

At the end of a long day of shooting, we pushed and hauled each other up the stone steps of the Château Borghese, laboured up to our rooms, bathed, dressed (much thought was bestowed on this rite) and went down to sit at our table, where the evening menu was curled in every glass. We had shed our anonymous costumes (CLEAN or DIRTY) and became birds, shells, tropical fish; each of us had developed her own pattern of stripes, spots, brilliant or subdued colours. The most spectacularly dressed were the two who had worn uniforms all their lives, Edna in her hospital and Catherine in her convent life. Now they burst into colour, along with the rest of us, and Michelle appeared in shining satin, in velvet that winked and shimmered with sequins and sparkles.

Most of the Château Borghese had been commandeered for us but the clientele for whom it was built were young couples who become starry-eyed at the thought of the bridal suite and are too preoccupied by love and sport to notice the Château Borghese's peculiarities. Though we were the pampered darlings of Angelo and Margaret, we noticed that they sometimes made up the entire staff or that in their absence the telephone at the front desk might ring forlornly for ten minutes at a time and finally give up. At mealtimes, Monique, the blond waitress who was in a perpetual state of puzzlement, tried to untangle anglophone orders, reheat vegetables, change fish for a hamburger or rice for potatoes. There was a certain informality of service suitable for those who were paying reduced rates, but sometimes real guests came and sat apart at tables with candles and flowers, while a tuxedo-clad waiter hovered and made suggestions in the grand manner. If the table of old ladies laughing (even whistling like birds at times) seemed odd to them, it was explained to them that we were in an NFB semi-documentary, and when we left the dining room, we bowed politely to each other.

We fell in love with the Château Borghese. To me, it was our ship; we were passengers who walked the clanging corridors to our staterooms, each closing: shur-cluck, followed by a firm clack as we locked ourselves into the only place where we could be entirely alone with our thoughts. On days of baking heat the trees outside stood motionless, the birds were silent, Margaret's frail marigolds keeled over and died. At night not a breath of air came through my open window and I lay on my bed jerking and twitching with insomnia, after the day's intensity and with the prospect of an early wake-up call. A feature of the summer—insomnia; too much excitement, too much fatigue, or when it was cool, drugged sleep under the quilted bedspread, and vivid dreams.

The Château Borghese was our fourth location, and despite our carping we came to love its rhythms and eccentricities. It was one of the places where a parallel development was happening along with the semi-documentary, at our long cheerful table in the dining room, in our comings and goings and greetings and farewells, even our solitary confinement in our rooms. At the gala dinners when the menu was printed in three languages, with smoked filet of shad, la crème Andalouse, vitello limone, when dinner began with kir and ended with Margarita dolce. Catherine sat at the end of the table out on the terrace, dressed in red from head to toe; she was drawn to the upright piano (moved out for the occasion), her hands raced over the keyboard, she burst into song. It was as giddy as any ocean voyage, and without even knowing it we were working out the groundwork (or the heartwork) of the semi-documentary, until by the time of the gala dinner our Château Borghese selves and our film selves were interchangeable.

MINIATURE: DAVID WILSON

One night at the Château Borghese, an unfamiliar person appeared in the doorway of the dining room, stood motionless and vanished. It was David Wilson, producer and co-editor with Cynthia of the film, someone whispered, and our heads turned in his direction only to find that he was gone. His expression of anxious gloom seemed to contain the question: could he edit this unlikely group of old women into a viable film? I felt that we were unloved, and saw us as what we were, the most unpromising material for the box office. When he reappeared later in the summer wearing a half-smile I simplistically translated it into approval. Gloria, meantime, had been puffing up like an indignant owl and darkly muttering, and I squeezed out of her (she was extremely discreet about any suggestion of discord) that David did not quite share her faith and that the budget, through miscalculation in financial quarters, as it turned out, had suddenly shrunk. David's half-smile corresponded to the return of the budget to its projected state of health, which included two more weeks of filming in September. Between David's two looks lay a period of anxiety, during which everything went on for us as usual, and we basked in the same benevolent atmosphere.

March 2, 1991. Cynthia tells me that her real work with David on the film started in November, 1988. I ask her whether Gloria shared in the work of editing. "Gloria came to the assembly screening," says Cynthia. It was just at this time that Gloria was told that she had a shadow on her lung and was unable to continue at the Film Board. From then on, the editing was done by Cynthia, with her vision of what the film was about, and David, puzzled by thirty hours of footage that did not seem to be about anything, dubious about the two of them finding a structure for it, dubious about his own role. "A complicated collaboration," says Cynthia. Over and over again they viewed each scene, David with his "extraordinary technique, his skill with hands and brain," and Cynthia, with her vision of "chances to make it live." "We did have to play," she says. It was "a symphony orchestra." I see her as a conductor who, after many rehearsals, brings a symphony to life. David, she says, was "more and more devoted." Yet even when they had cut all the scenes and had done the final editing, he was still puzzled. "It's all wonderful," he said, "but is it a movie?" Gloria's scenario had suggested a "story," but this film had been taken by the wayward movements of the cast away from and beyond the "story" to an unanticipated place where it wanted to live. Cynthia knew that eventually our million molecules would reveal *the* meaning; David made the molecules work together.

"Stubborn and shy," Cynthia says about David. At the Château Borghese David kept his eyes averted from the table where we, the flesh-and-blood members of the cast, were eating our dinner. Was it shyness, or might we have distracted him from the concentration he needed to look objectively at our myriad film-images? In public he seems to be holding himself together in order to guard his inner life, to be reluctant to share it, to have an exacerbated sense of the banality of small talk. He seems to inhabit a room of his own, and to close the door more firmly when he is surrounded by people.

INTERVAL

Peter (to Patrick, laying a hand on his arm):
Did you see an old woman going down the
path?

Patrick: I did not, but I saw a young girl,
and she had the walk of a queen.

—*CATHLEEN NI HOULIHAN*, W. B. YEATS

Well before dawn the blue tents like Morpho butterflies begin
their flight, choose a landing place on rough grass still soggy
with dew; they are set up and pegged; tables, a refrigerator, a
coffee machine materialize, food is spread on a long table, two
Jiggs toilets hover and land at a discreet distance; the gazebo
with its groundcloth and chaises longues flies in, ready for one
of us to rest under its softly billowing roof. The vans full of
equipment are lined up side by side, or trunk to tail like circus
elephants, in a field below an abandoned house. Our own route
to the location takes us endlessly up and down hills and around
bends. We are already steeped in the magic of the grey van, with
the laughter, song, games it generates even at seven a.m., the
attention to outside details, new or familiar, a stretch of giant
sunflowers, a bloated cow lying on her side, the hump of her
belly like a grey rock in the mist. Is she dead? Edna knows what

to do about a cow bloated with wet grass—you stick a knife into her side and the gas escapes.

The day of the bloated cow we come to an open gate and a narrow road that leads downward as steeply as a ski jump; we take off, dive down, wind through primeval forest, past trees hung with pale moss, rocks huddled under viridian capes. The sun shines through a hole in the canopy and makes a spotlit circle on the road, in which stands Cynthia, wearing her grey-green jumpsuit, the colour of the forest, her long hair falling over her shoulders. "Beautiful, beautiful," we all murmur. "Umph," says Gloria. Cynthia is guiding us to the place where the tents, the food, the Jiggses, have descended apparently without human intervention.

We are spectators and recipients in the great magic show. Disembodied hands holding styrofoam cups appear just as the words *water* or *coffee* form in a head; invisible spirits place chairs under our bums (Cissy's word) just before we fall backward into space, or coats on our backs, or scarves around our necks on a nippy morning. The same hands are also held out to be draped with the same coats, scarves, extraneous handbags and hats, to be hidden in secret places, away from the camera's prying eye. Umbrellas, parasols, bee helmets materialize, according to the weather. On hot, still days we stand knee-deep in meadow grass, looking like extraterrestrials, helmeted in green gauze while the black flies peer in greedily from outside. Through a green mist I see us lined up, eight mediaeval women warriors, waiting for our marching orders.

As for the human beings responsible for all the practical magic, they are there at the ends of roads, the tops of hills, beside the lake, or they have climbed up the face of a cliff, always ahead of us, looking as though it is the most natural thing in the world to get a wake-up call at three a.m. in the pitch dark, to hurry through breakfast at the Rivière Rouge. One human being has got up even earlier than the crew to get breakfast ready—Nicole, round and rosy, with magical good spirits like sunbeams radiating from every pore. Even at seven-thirty when we straggle in, she is still charged with goodwill and can hold ten different orders in her head. Women more or less like Nicole, sisters of Hera or the corn goddess, are in every one of our hostels: the Château Borghese, the Rivière Rouge, the Town Hall at Huberdeau. Men providers, too, appear on a hilltop with pita bread sandwiches stuffed with fresh crabmeat, or burst into an old Québecois song or a jig, if the occasion requires. In ordinary life there are few occasions that require, certainly not several in a single day. And the word *require* is too stern to suggest what occasions do there, for they break open like a milkweed pod and scatter shining silk filaments in every direction.

All of this is from *our* point of view, the eight of us who are treated like royalty, queens for the summer, while the film army and the supply corps toil and sweat from dawn to dark and beyond, stand motionless for untold hours, or heave things from here to there countless times in a day, and fall into bed so exhausted that they will never catch up the lost hours of sleep. No wonder they look pale and grim sometimes and we hear a low rumble like an imminent earthquake, combined with the sharp snap of a temper. As queens, we ignore all signs of stress except our own. Until the day when the set becomes suddenly dark, the snaky cables slither away, the cameras, lamps, drop sheets, sandbags and assorted paraphernalia withdraw silently. "OK, that's it," says Cynthia shortly. Shooting resumes after a decent interval, a weekend, time to allow tempers to cool and bodies to renew their forces, arbitration, negotiation, etc. We, the cast, are in such a fairyland that visible disharmony takes us by surprise. It is as though we have looked through the peephole of a curtain that separates us from the serious world, *their* world where authentic human emotions flourish: impatience, arguments, sexism, desires and frustrations of every description, the fear (watching the hourglass) that time or money will run out. And who knows how they feel about us? It is part of semi-documentary film etiquette not to betray by a happy smile or a twitching of the mouth or a sudden rise of voice decibels, what you think of a given scene. Occasionally Cynthia utters the single word, "Good" (differently inflected according to enthusiasm?) and we grab at the word like greedy carp. Sometimes she claps her hands with a rhythmic silent clapping, and this, it is said by minute observers, means Bad. A word of praise or criticism might precipitate us over the top, or to a bottomless effort of repetition, or an analysis (ours) of what we should do to be "good." If a scene is repeated five times, it isn't necessarily because we are doing it badly; there are practical reasons related to all filmmaking: perhaps it is because a hair or a black fly has lodged on the camera lens, or the light has changed, or, now and then, I admit, because one of us has got too close to the camera. The reaction to our real lapses is patient resignation; not once do we suffer the humiliations of professional actresses. That, too, is magic, the medium of downy nonjudgement we live in. Constance and I, who spend our time looking for ways to blame ourselves, are hard put to find pretexts. And isn't that one of the reasons for our happiness?

In reality, we are seven old women and a young woman. People look curiously at us as we file into the Rivière Rouge for lunch, or they stare openly at us, for we look to them just like seven old women, some of us not entirely steady on our feet. And what are we doing there? One day, after three oafish, unshaven men in checked shirts and muddy boots have been too engrossed in staring even to drink their beer, Winnie says wryly, "I wanted to say to them, 'What are you staring at? Haven't you ever seen film stars before?'" The three men didn't know that we were film stars disguised as old women; they didn't have the magic power to penetrate our disguise any more than Papageno has in *The Magic Flute* when Papagena appears disguised as a gabbling crone.

Some of the magic is prodigally bestowed on us by nature; one of us may look carelessly out on the way home and see something so portentous that Alison will have to stop the van so that we can all look. Such a vision is the Great Rock, scarcely visible in the shade of the trees and underbrush surrounding it. It is a granite diamond, fully thirty feet high, balanced on one of its points; it has been there since the Ice Age. From that day on, coming or going, one of us will say, "We're getting near the Great Rock." Often I say it; I can feel its emanations; it will be around the next bend, not far from a little dirt road and a blue mailbox with W. PARTRIDGE printed in white letters on it. It is always a shock to hear Gloria or Alison say, "We passed it long ago."

Catching sight of the Great Rock is a solemn occasion like hearing a huge gong struck once. It is the rock of ages, but a tree is growing from a crack on its side; perhaps in time, the tree will split it apart. The rock, the double rainbows, the full moon rising, the giant horse that appears from nowhere, the jumping mice and the singing coyotes—these are our big symbols (of what, we are never sure); they are on the edge of film-time, complementing it and making us aware of the magic that goes into the making of every scene. "Alice is beginning to understand the art of illusion in filmmaking," says Cynthia one day, when Alice suggests that I score little cuts on our one and only apple to get the actual cutting (by me with my inch-long Swiss pocket knife) over more quickly. We become good at suspending disbelief; the chicken legs that we devour out on the porch are really the legs of the tiny chirruping frogs we've caught and have unwillingly killed; the enormous cultivated blueberries and raspberries we eat have been picked in the fields; the desiccated mushrooms Cissy and I find with cries of delight were really growing in the woods. In fact, they have been artfully stuck into the moss and arranged on a tree stump by a Catholic brother, who has appeared with a tin box and reverently extracted the mushrooms, which he uses on his guided nature walks. This brother has the shape of a very tall, elongated bird, and a gentle, crafty look. We talk about birds. He has seen a huge one this spring, he says, red all over. What can it be? I suggest a scarlet tanager, "un tanagra," but point out that it's smaller than a robin and has black wings. "Oui, oui, un tanagra!" he cries, "mais c'était deux fois plus grand." He belongs to the race of birdwatchers who claim to have seen the impossible: a sky-blue hummingbird, something bright pink, or something twice life-size, who enrage more humdrum people like me to the point of inexcusable rudeness.

The season changes from summer to autumn; wild mushrooms actually poke up all over the place, and Cissy and I have an authentic mushroom scene. Nature is wheedled and cajoled and, sometimes, does the filmmakers' bidding; it rains when they want rain, though more likely, rain comes sluicing over the roof from a hose, or a genuine downpour puts an abrupt end to the filming. David and Roger, the cameramen, patiently watch a little blue patch of sky and wait for the sun to break through, or vice versa, or a big cloud seems to pick us to dump on when the rest of the landscape is bathed in golden light. This unanticipated phenomenon delights me. We are waiting down near the lake, shadow and sunlight moving over the field; when the hot sun hits us, hands hold parasols over our heads, segmented blue and yellow, blue and red, a flowered one, the green-grey one with its dove-grey shade. A cloud poised over us suddenly rains down its rain, which falls in a shining circle around the overlapping umbrellas where we cluster together like stalagmites. Sally, holding the red and blue umbrella, is wearing her grey, shiny boots like Christopher Robin's, baggy striped blue and white shorts, a lilac-coloured tee shirt and a fuchsia pen on a string around her neck.

Sally has trained horses, ridden in shows and to hounds, is one of those superior beings (first-class riders) who make my heart flutter. Horses, it turns out, are part of the magic at the film's edge; one evening we see a chestnut mare and her golden foal standing under a double rainbow in a bright green field. It is Sally who quickly knots a piece of ordinary white string and slips it over the head of the giant horse who has come plodding down the road, who is going to plod dreamily right into the back of our yellow bus. Surprised by Sally's authority, he comes to a full stop and waits until a black-haired, black-eyed young man appears glowering and muttering. *Our* horse. He has a wide white blaze on his face and splayed-out hooves. We stand watching his big rump getting smaller as the angry young man leads him away.

The day of the horse, in the damp woods where the moss is phosphorescent and the deer-foot fungus climb up the tree trunks, was full of signs, loaded with meanings beyond perception like the Great Rock. A pale toad, motionless in the soft groundcover, with an owl's staring face drawn in India ink on its back, a green skull, almost buried in the moss, with snow-white teeth. And another day, the day of the jumping mice, a sad story transformed into comedy. Rubber boots trampling their kingdom under the long grass, sharp tripod legs suddenly piercing their nests. In their panic they take flight upward; catapulted by their long back legs, exquisite in their satiny green-gold coats. In the melee one of them has had its leg broken and falls on its side. Sally picks it up and hands it to a crew member noted for her compassion. Hasn't she stroked the head of a monstrous bullfrog? She takes the mouse by the tail and sends it sailing over the field. Later, Gloria and I dissolve into helpless laughter when Gloria says, "I hadn't expected her to make a little splint for it, but . . . ." The little splint, the impossible test of compassion like the senseless tests in fairytales. The jumping mice have made their invisible kingdom under the very spot where the big boots *have* to trample, where tripod legs *have* to pierce. Down by the lake another population is hidden; a host of tiny frogs in the water below the marsh grass hop up like fleas if you step off the boardwalk. At least fifty of them are caught, and star in a scene in the house, chirruping in a white enamel pot covered with a dishcloth. "Oh gawd!" cries Alice, stepping back, for some of the frogs have hopped clear up to the edge and are peering out. Alice, who had to cut off frogs' legs when she was a child, developed frogophobia. The rest of us are supposed to be so hungry that we're ready to kill and eat them. We don't, we won't. Winnie and I take the enamel pot down to the marsh and tip it sideways on the boardwalk. Dazed, the little frogs sit for a moment before leaping into their marshy homeland.

The turning point, the moment when disbelief is suspended and magic can happen. Like falling into the uncritical but attentive happiness of love. Everything is perfect; everything is beautiful. It had something to do with understanding the art of illusion. The magic apple, the magicification of every living and growing thing, including ourselves, who were radiant film stars disguised as old women. Now we are ourselves again and almost two years older. Gloria, our jester, is dead. The Cissy who was part of the film's magic has had a stroke and has retired into a Cissy whose memories of the film are uncertain, and the rest of us are back in our pre-film lives. In Montreal, magic isn't prodigally bestowed but has to be dug out of the day, like a truffle from the earth under an oak tree.

T H E   M E N

Men were there, underpinning the filming. It took me at least a week to begin to distinguish them as faces, as bodies, or according to the clothes they wore, rumpled or carefully chosen: a clean striped shirt, new creased khaki pants or shorts from which extended legs of all sorts—bony, hairy, stalwart. I did not really look at them, or only obliquely, fleetingly, averting my eyes, even when David de Volpi, the Director of Photography, was an inch away from my head with his light meter, careful always not to look at me directly but at a place beyond me, in the same way that I was pretending not even to notice that he was there so close. He was sensitive to our almost imperceptible flinching away from this invasion of our privacy; the pale eye of the light meter, held next to my white head, saw me in strange new terms, saw this big mass of whiteness as a problem and would inform David of its magnitude. David understood via the light meter that my head had to be subdued or its elements differentiated. He had mastered the art of lighting, in which everything had its own luminescence, without undue emphasis on a blaze of white. Like the Creator on Day One he could call for sunshine or moonlight, turn afternoon into twilight and vice versa. But that first day I had not thought about any of this, only felt the cold fish's eye of the light meter grazing my head and the great luminous eyes of the cameras across the room, with a man waiting beside each one (David and Roger Martin), staring at me, reducing me to an image, colours, mostly pink and white, which were part of the total composition on which it was focussed. As time went on, David himself came into focus: his handsome, straight-nosed, blue-eyed face, trim body, beautiful blue-striped or denim shirts (as often as not my eye would land on his shirt rather than his face), and it gradually came to me that in the name of light and the temperament of the cameras, which were as finicky as thoroughbreds lined up at the gate, he had the power of veto. "I can't do that," he would say, meaning, "The cameras won't do that." The cameras obeyed David, looked at David when Cynthia gave them a command; the authority of David and the cameras were so intertwined, in fact, that it was hard to tell which of them was doing the refusing.

There were other men there who couldn't or wouldn't be pushed an inch beyond their sense of the possible: Jacques Drouin, the roly-poly one with a voice like a town crier's and a laugh that could be heard echoing against the distant hills, rumbled at times volcanic rumblings of dire warning. He had an acute sense of time and its contractual boundaries, and it was understandable if his brows knitted when he had been up since four a.m. and the sun set on wrap-time. He and the other members of the crew had their vetoes, too; they could turn off the lights in the middle of a scene, and with dark, determined looks, relentlessly start the wrapping process, while we, ever willing to do the impossible, hardly knew whether to feel dismay or relief. It was certain that the men exerted power from their place behind the scene; was it because they were men, who unwittingly ooze manpower, manwill, even when women are at the helm and men compose about half of the crew? Or did they have legitimate reasons for exercising their veto? Would an all-female crew have done the same? We like to think that all would have been harmony and joyful acquiescence if an all-female crew had been asked to do the impossible, to work longer hours than their contract called for, etc. Of course we considered all such matters from our prideful point of view as a willing and infinitely enduring cast; we were flattered by all the attention we got from the luminous camera eyes, by David with his impersonal intent gaze and extra fish-eye, by Jacques with his furry mike held aloft as if he were a pole vaulter about to take off, by the inordinate amount of time it took to set things up for *us*, by the beautiful young women scurrying around with heavy equipment on their shoulders or dragging or pushing; they were bronzed and muscular as Amazons, these slaves of manpower. Did they share in the manmade rebellion at times? It was impossible to read their minds; we were all too busy for the leisure activity of reading minds even when we were in a passive state of waiting, though flashes of anger, the complicity of this person with that person, the exertion of manwill, a lurking gladness (in Him) if He could say it can't be done, his thought made visible—that only a woman could think it *could* be done—all these like little flashing movements seen out of the corner of an eye. A feeling, justified by the turning off of the lights, the pulling-together of Jacques' black eyebrows and his stomping off with the look of one who has to be wooed and cajoled, his manly feelings soothed before he will come back.

It was for the most part a discreet and hidden battle of the sexes, carried on in the magnetic field of sexual vibrations. Does this always happen to cloud the crystal-clear purpose of a film project made in high summer, and change the chemistry of coexisting bodies determinedly impersonal? Men's bodies hovered over us or we brushed them in passing; they were not deliberately sending out signals; indeed, they seemed to be suppressing the usual signals, though I have to remind myself that our age (65 to 88) was certainly a deterrent to signals; men don't usually flirt with women old enough to be their grandmothers. Women, on the other hand, *do* flirt with men young enough to be their grandsons. At the Château Borghese, if a man sat down at our table, there was a flurry of cooing. François Gingras, in particular, who looks so much like Marcus Aurelius, with his curly hair just slightly receding from a noble forehead, and his Roman nose and fine chiselled mouth, triggered schoolgirlish flirting. I was guilty in my own way of what might be called negative flirting, of not seeming to give a damn about François' body, charged with involuntary sex appeal, which stood in such casually manly attitudes. He must have been sick to death of being an automatic object of admiration, for his aloofness was different from any other man's and this aloofness was the driving force of his magnetism, which I believe drew every one of us of whatever age into a covert study of him, or found open expression in the aforesaid cooing. It made me reflect on the silly helplessness of women in the presence of men.

Not that it surprised me. Hadn't my own mother, when I was still paralyzed by shyness and reluctantly going to my first dances, suggested first steps toward the capture of a man by drawing him out? In due time I mastered the bright attentive look, the judicious word to insert in some little chink in *his* discourse; I learned that it was easy to prime the conversational pump: it simply required a little arrangement of the face in an expression of friendly interest, a settling of limbs for the duration. Women talk too, you say. True, I have heard many a droning wife and seen her husband looking expressionlessly into space. But his mind is not tuned to hers as hers is to his; he does not have the durably attentive look. He is neither looking nor listening; he has gone into a state somewhat like hibernation; less blood is going to his brain, only enough to frame the words, "Yes, dear," or "Yes, I am," if she says, "You're not listening." He has learned that an absolute minimum of attention will suffice to keep her from becoming dangerously angry. At the Château Borghese I observed our transformation from autonomous beings to creatures programmed to react in the time-honoured way to men—a magic change from an old to a young woman, who pats the seat of the empty chair next to her. "Sit by me," she says to some male crew member who has chanced to stray into the spiderweb of our table. She places one elbow on the table and her head, winsomely tipped, on her hand. She turns toward him with that special smile that says, "Speak! I'm listening."

It took me a while to distinguish one member of the crew from another and to realize that unlike other species of men, each was entirely different from the other. Film people are like musicians; they can't be recognized by any sameness of clothes or features, and can be roughly classified as artists. Pierre Pouliot, the special effects magician, *was* an artist, a writer. The steam of a big book had been building in him for years and now he was ready to let it out. He wore a battered hat and rumpled clothes and rollicked around like a half-grown puppy. He was a birdwatcher, felt reverence for all of nature, would appear with his hands cupped over a patriarchal bullfrog or a jumping mouse with a broken leg. It was he who brought a big orphan puppy on the set, later to be Gloria's Molly. A sheepdog? Afghan? Irish wolfhound? All of us speculated according to the vast size of her paws. With his artist's eye Pierre produced effects, special and otherwise: he knew where to find mushrooms and could make a nature morte out of a few blueberries and raspberries on a big green leaf. He could make smoke by heaping damp grass over a little twig fire. He was full of fantasy and a great desire to reveal his inner world, and the feminine tenderness peculiar to a sub-group of men, whose voices are soft and caressing.

Another of these gentle creatures whom I liked to look at

(covertly) was Raynald Lavoie, who looked in his emaciated state startlingly like Donatello's Maddalena, even if she is fifty years older and clad only in her own long hair. Raynald is tall, bony, hollow-cheeked like la Maddalena, and his hair falls over his forehead. On the set he was so informed by the sacredness of his mission as crew member, and so shy that we never exchanged a single word or look until the filming was almost over; he was driven by the intense wish to do things right, would fly by, looking neither to right nor left, with some piece of equipment. A vision of him lingers in my head: a hot day in August, at the lake location. Cissy and I are sitting on a rock in the hot sun; in front of us, mushrooms, all found in the woods, have been beautifully arranged by Pierre on a cedar branch laid over a board. We are waiting for the camera to be set up. The sun is beating down, and Raynald, with each booted foot placed on a small rock, the water lapping idly over them, is holding up a pale green silk umbrella that casts a translucent shade over us. He is wearing shorts and socks, is in his state of aloof intentness. I wake up that night thinking of the dazzle and soft, greenish shade, and the bony young man, very seriously holding the umbrella aloft, while Cissy picks absently at the mushrooms and blows on them to get the earth off.

And then a final vision at the Film Board. Raynald is there and I greet him joyfully. A great smile breaks out on his face, a great twisting shyness possesses his limbs. I want to clasp him in my arms—two equally skinny bodies embracing. Shy people recognize each other from set movements, the choreography of shyness; our bodies obey mysterious orders to cast down our eyes and to lose control of our feet, to leave the scene with a headlong rush; we have a burning sensation of eyes fixed on our backs like cattle prods. Maybe Raynald doesn't know it but we are bound together in the fellowship of sometimes uncontrollable shyness, like a stutter that possesses the whole body.

INTERVAL

... What boots it to repeat
How Time is slipping underneath our Feet:
Unborn TO-MORROW and dead YESTERDAY.
Why fret about them if TO-DAY be sweet!

—EDWARD FITZGERALD,
RUBÁIYÁT OF OMAR KHAYYÁM

Slack-water, the period between tides, slack-time, waitlessness. Our school bus is stopped out in the field enclosed in fog; we are sitting in silence waiting for the signal for Michelle to start the bus. We will roll through fog, down a hill, and disappear from the view of the camera. In the course of shooting, reshooting, the sun comes up and gradually rolls the fog toward the edge of the field where it lies like a long satin ribbon, floats a hilltop on a white pillow, sharpens the outlines of distant spruce-steeples, puffs up the maples, glinting with autumn (it is September 10th, our last day), sends slanting pink veils of fog over mountains, trees and down to the drenched grass. The crew stands in the damp stillness with the sun on their backs and their hands in their pockets. The camera waits.

Time has no gravity in waitlessness, does not pull you from second to second into the future. In the beginning I am a slave

PENTICTON PUBLIC LIBRARY

to watch-time. "Sometimes I think an hour has gone by," I say in my journal. "I look at my watch and it's only ten minutes." Little by little I learn to unhitch certain terminals in my brain that compel me to glance down at my wrist, where a second hand is hopping its way around the face of my watch. I begin to float in time. July 7th: "I've lost track of minutes, of hours, of morning and afternoon, of the day itself. The day is eternal; it's like being high over the earth as it turns, in eternal daylight."

We are at Location II; the lake is glassy, scarcely ruffled, a burning sun is diffused through the clouds. There are trance-like silences, two crew members move across the mirror of the lake on a raft pushed by a tiny silent motor. The hours are pulled out, as fine as spider-silk.

"If you'd kept on good terms with time," says the Mad Hatter to Alice, "He'd do almost anything you liked with the clock." Time for filmmakers stands still or runs backwards, moves the end to the beginning, the future before the past. They are magicians. Everybody knows this except me, it seems, for I am struck with delight when we are shown a first version of the film and the apple we have cut up and eaten reappears, whole, in a later scene. An oversight, of course. For me it was a magic apple, the symbol of *us*, who started in pieces and came together as a whole. I was sorry that the recomposed apple had to be cut out, a victim of clock-time, which now and then asserted itself in the editing room. But . . . "you should have cut it into eight pieces," says Sally, "we all forgot that. In the end nobody noticed." Nobody noticed the liberties taken by time and logic, which would have been pounced on in any other kind of film. Finally, not even the things that had seemed so important out there—correctness decreed by clock-time: the length, the colour of hair, for instance, were among the things not noticed. Perhaps only the apple and our clothes (marked CLEAN and DIRTY on their garment bags) belonged to clock-time; our clothes had a clean before, and an after of grease stains (Catherine), mud stains (Michelle), grass stains (Alice). They show that time has passed, but how much? How many days and nights go by? The hours seem to be stalled in some kind of magic circularity. Perhaps it was in obedience to this concept of circularity or stillness of time that a scene in which Catherine is rubbing castor oil on her feet, in preparation for her thirty-kilometre trek to get help, was temporarily cut, and our little rescue plane simply comes down from the sky with Catherine aboard. "I did it!" she cries, and we are left to imagine what she did. The editors have assumed that the audience is capable of making leaps of imagination by filling in the open spaces of time, that they don't need a spoon-fed narrative. When Sally says, "In the end, nobody noticed," she means that nobody noticed what didn't matter. Ordinary time stops when our bus dies; the bus was a vehicle for carrying us forward, to an appointed time in an appointed place, and now we are held in slack-time, spellbound. The story of the film is the story of the eight pieces of us coming together, an invisible and motionless progress, a gravity pulling toward the still centre that is the place of art.

Certainly it was not planned, the mutual spin-off between off- and on-camera in slack-time, which couldn't have happened without taking us away from our city lives and putting us together in a melting pot. The three fates must have watched our melting with fascinated surprise, how it was happening both off and on. Though they couldn't see that a "story" was developing until they watched the rushes, saw that what was going on off-camera was being translated (a kind of sign language?) into our film selves. The Château Borghese (one of the unfilmed locations) mirrors the circularity of the film. The end of the day is the beginning in reverse; at the crack of dawn we sidle carefully down the stone steps of the Château Borghese, hanging on to each other, someone below to form a human cushion in case of need; at the end, in the fading light, we help each other up. Silences, perhaps, at both beginning and end, a few heartfelt groans, expressions that speak volumes. These are all part of the language that forges tiny new bonds between sunrise and sunset, that speaks of a consensus, of assent.

B E T H

Beth has the tidy, trim look of a white-throated sparrow (the bird whose song haunts Constance) and her plumage has the same colours: brown, black, white, grey, with a touch of yellow. She is the only one of us whose film costume seems entirely appropriate. She holds herself very straight; she wobbles a little on the needly heels of her slender pumps, but she can walk a mile or so and stand for hours without getting tired, she says. Or she can wait as we all waited out on the location, to be in a scene that didn't materialize, sometimes all day long. I felt the intensity of her waiting, for she was almost motionless; she wasn't sprawled out or carelessly sitting like some of us but was always perfectly posed, with one knee crossed over the other, with the ghost of a smile on her face. I felt torment building in her, and I imagined a hundred reasons for it but (at first) not the right one—that her whole being was concentrated on her wish to act, for hadn't they said to her after her try-outs, "Beth, you were *great!*" Hadn't that meant that at last, at the age of 80, she would come into her own, the actress-self she had yearned for a lifetime to be, felt in herself, and seemed now to be inexplicably muzzled?

I assumed that Beth's intense stillness was the result of the tragedies in her life, which she was gradually recounting to me: the deaths of her favourite sister, her first husband, and her only son. I imagined the mainspring of her life stopping the day her son died. "People get excited about things," she said to me the day she told me about her son's death, "and I think, how can they be so excited?" After the film is over, when I am interviewing her, I start by saying, "I remember your saying you were lonely." "I said I was *lonely?*" she exclaims indignantly. "I'm not lonely. No! I *like* being by myself. I love my life now because there's no man in it, you see . . . . And I have my radio programs and my TV and my books and I'm always cooking and shopping. I love to eat . . . . My life is filled with just me." So much for my impressions, I think. I had persisted in my false idea of Beth's loneliness because it corresponded to her habit of holding herself still and apart, waiting to be spoken to. I only gradually discovered that inside the quiet person there was a Beth ready to burst into eager speech, or to leap up and start dancing the Charleston or singing a slightly bawdy song from the '30s or '40s.

Novelists can deduce people's lives from the outside; I can't and should know better than to try. Would a novelist have guessed the place men have had in Beth's life? That she had lost—in one way or another—three husbands? The first died slowly of cancer, the second was a madman, the third a compulsive gambler. One of her suitors shot himself; "I don't know whether he shot himself for me or because he was a failure in life," she says. In between times, countless men passed like shooting stars through her life, not without making pests of themselves, however: phoning, insisting, arguing. Just after she'd signed the divorce papers so that the gambler could marry another hapless woman, he asked her to have lunch with him. "If you'd just say the word, I'd marry you again tomorrow," he said. And three years ago a "very handsome" man kept after her until she told him no, that she was too old. "I don't want to get tied up with another man," she told him, and to me she said, "That was the last romance, if you can call it a romance. I think he was a loser, too." In the course of the interview I'm wonderstruck by Beth's ability to catch men. In photographs of her as a young woman, she is a dark-haired beauty with an oval face, an irresistibly flirtatious smile. I'd seen this smile at the Château Borghese, felt electromagnetic waves pulse through the atmosphere into the body of any man who happened into their field. A perpetual surprise to me, the energy that women who like men can emit. "When did you start being interested in boys?" I ask her after she has told me about the "last romance." "Well, I was about ten," she says. He was a boy named Percy Fox, who walked by when she and her girlfriend, Doreen, were sitting on her front steps. "Do you want to hear a song I wrote about Percy Fox? 'Percy my darling/ Percy my own/ Jump up beside me/ And kiss me all alone/ I love you dearly/ I love you so/ Percy my darling/ Percy my own.' Imagine, at ten!" she adds gleefully.

"And now," she says, "my life is filled with just me." She is expanding into the space of "just me" after all these years of being a good wife who believed in the good wife's obligations as caretaker. But instead of rewarding her, life has dished out punishment. As her sister Lilly said, Beth's life has been one of "walking on stones." "More like walking on broken glass," I say. "But," I say, thinking suddenly that Beth's gift for enjoying life is like Constance's, "you were born to be happy." "Yes, I have a very happy nature," she answers. Both she and Constance were happy children, but were pummelled by cruelty, meanness, sickness and death. And, in Beth's case, dire poverty and war.

Out there on the various locations, at the Château Borghese and the Rivière Rouge and the Town Hall at Huberdeau, I can feel the vibration of Beth, not that of suffering or loneliness, after all, but of her great desire to tell me her story, to make her whole life exist as the film makes her exist as an actress. Now she is moved by my attention to share the burden of her life with me; we are bound together by mutual need, to be heard, to hear. One day she shows me a photograph of herself as a child, with her sisters and baby brothers. The sisters are wearing identical dresses made by their mother, of heavy, stiff material, skirts well below their knees, and high-buttoned boots. "Can you guess which is me?" I stare at them and identify Sophie, the eldest, with her feet planted apart and a mean, petulant look on her face. The pretty one is Beth. I am mesmerized by the child Beth, who contains her future life, who is the woman watching my reaction. At an age when I still looked and behaved like a baby, Beth looks sagacious and determined, she already has a mature *just me*, which is the same now as it was then, she is already aware of her power to charm, to become someone's pet.

Sometimes she asks me questions or gives me answers that twist my heart with sorrow. "Did I tell you that my son died?" "Did I tell you that I'm Jewish?" This is in the quiet of my house. "No, you didn't." "You didn't *know*?" She looks at me, sizes me up, how will I take it? Quite soon, I discover her shrewdness and her ability to size people up with a single glance. "Was it very hard for you when you were growing up?" I ask her. Yes, it was hard; the children used to run after her, crying, "Dirty Jew!" On another day: "Did I tell you that I wear a wig?" I didn't know this either; her short, tidy brown-grey hair fits so nicely over her forehead and around her ears. In one of her big scenes (did each of us have a scene that required an act of courage, one that would only be possible in that atmosphere of trust?) she takes off her wig with a decisive gesture, and then, more courageous still, she appears wigless for dinner at the Château Borghese. "Beth, you look wonderful!" everybody says. Without her wig she has a very high forehead and her eyes seem huge, bright and haunted. The next day Beth is wearing her wig again.

Little Beth in the photograph is destined to attract men, to leap into marriage and to survive. Men didn't scare her even if she hardly knew them; otherwise, how did she dare, at seventeen, to entrust her life to Mr. Amor, who had gone to Canada to look for a job, but not without extracting a promise from Beth to come and marry him when he asked her to. Poor Beth! For the letter came and she didn't want to go, but her mother, "dear, lovely lady that she was," said, "You can't do that! You promised him! You can always come back," she added prudently. My mother, too, would have been on the man's side and held Beth to her promise whether she was in love with Mr. Amor or not. Which she wasn't. "I knew that I didn't love him enough to marry him but he'd already made all the arrangements over there . . . ." So that was how she married her first husband, not quite sight unseen, since he'd taken her on outings in London, but unknown. Fortunately he was an honourable man, unlike the two subsequent ones. But she was bitterly homesick, missed her mother and cried so much that it got on Mr. Amor's nerves. "Would you like to go and visit your family?" he asked kindly.

To me, to marry even a man you know would be a fearful gamble, to put yourself in the power of a person twice as strong as you are, who from then on is there day and night with habits and exigencies that are sprung on you without warning. I have a feeling that Beth imposed her impeccable orderliness on all three husbands. But how about sex? Sex with Mr. Amor (that name pregnant with ironic meaning) was a shock, for it was Beth's first real sexual experience. "Bed wasn't too good; we didn't talk about it in those days," she says, "but later I talked about it and found out that not too many men know how to be good in bed." My mother, if she had ever let the word "bed" in that context cross her lips, would have said that it isn't of paramount importance. Mothers who belong to the old school still believe this for their daughters, in vain, I've observed. Character is what counts, my mother would have said. But Beth, who sizes people up so quickly, doesn't seem to have had an infallible instinct for character in husbands, for she fell into two disastrous marriages, the one with the gambler and the other with a man who nearly scared her to death. "Harold!" she said to him one day. "Sometimes your eyes are so nice and clear; other times they look cloudy and when they're cloudy you're very quiet." Harold put his hands around her neck and said, "You're very trusting, aren't you?" Beth, who must be like quicksilver when she's cornered, made a getaway and phoned Harold's sister. "You know, Beth," said the sister, "we loved you so much we thought you'd be good for him." They loved Beth so much that they hadn't breathed a word about Harold's psychotic states and his frequent disappearances into mental institutions. ("Those places," Beth calls them.) "Wasn't that a terrible thing to have done to me?"

It wasn't as though Beth had had admirable male role models when she was growing up. "He didn't *drink*," she says about her father, a cabinetmaker, "I mean it wasn't drink that made him that way," i.e. heavy as lead when he came home from work, picking on everybody in the family, so that the "atmosphere was dull and miserable." And yet Beth was his favourite child. "That's why he used to take me to band concerts [which she hated] and I felt that I should do everything he asked me." This is the stranglehold that abusive men of whatever kind have over children. About the man who abused her when she was eight, Beth says, "I didn't want to upset him so that he wouldn't give me any more work to take to my mother. That was the whole thing, you see, to make the extra money. I have to think about it," she says, "I mean how can a man abuse a child? But they do; they have no feeling."

"Well, I'm not going to say that he was a vicious man," she says. "He tried the best way he could, he was bad enough to do what he *did*, if you want to call that vicious, I mean he wasn't going to hold me down." Besides, the man's father was upstairs and might hear, luckily for little Beth. But somehow her mother understood what had happened without Beth's saying a word, and sent her brother, two years younger, with the load of pillowcases the mother had sewed. Beth laughs merrily, for she is thinking not of the possible manhandling of her little brother, but of the amazing quickness, cleverness and retentive memories of little children and of all the things they did in those days (and these days, too—more millions of child-slaves in grimy factories than when Beth was young).

But no need to worry about little Beth, as intrepid as my miniature Pekingese, Winky. Winky would stand her ground in front of a presumptuous Great Dane and fly at his throat if necessary. Beth, who looks so fragile, is no more fragile than a piece of steel tempered by fire. She's tough and resilient and afraid of nothing, except perhaps the wail of coyotes or the whispering sounds of night in the country. She's a creature of the city, toughened by her life as a child on the street. "I always felt that playing in the street is a kind of education," I say. "We were *not* allowed to play in the street." "I think you were deprived," says Beth with a laugh. She tells me how, shy as she was, she used to fight her little brother's street battles. "If I saw anything starting I'd put them down." "With your fists?" "*Jumping* on them; I'd *jump on them.*" I try to imagine the child Beth in her high-buttoned boots jumping on a boy twice her size and beating him up. She is made of tempered steel, clever, sharp-tongued, with a memory like a computer. A little hellion at school, so naughty that she was caned by the headmistress. Beth was the ringleader of the Fearless Three: herself, Esther Berman and Bella Munro. "If you were *very* naughty you got two-handers on each hand, two cane-strikes, and your name in a black book." I shiver with horror, but Beth didn't care a hoot about her name in the black book, nor did she tell her mother, except for one time "when I thought I didn't deserve the cane."

Beth refined her arts of defence as she went along, even knew how to flee from a deranged husband. She survived by her wits, her quickness. Yet she seemed to throw herself headlong into marriage more or less the way she rushed unseeing toward the dance platform at the Rivière Rouge and fell like Icarus from the sky. Better to be rash than manless, however. Society decrees that a woman *has* to have a man and that if she loses one she must immediately begin looking for another. So her instinct drives her just as it drives a bird to choose a mate—"a good catch," as Mr. Amor was, the bird with the brightest crest, the most impressive nuptial dance and the look of the one who will work hard at the onerous job of feeding the nestlings. Love isn't necessarily a priority. "My mother said you can love a man who's good to you even if you don't love him now." This was when she was propelling Beth across the ocean to marry Mr. Amor. Exactly what *my* mother said on a similar occasion! There must be a little red book of phrases for mothers that they commit to memory. Mr. Amor, luckily, turned out to be a "good" husband and was the father of their son, a beautiful boy who became a gifted musician and died of meningitis; he had Beth's oval face and dark eyes. It was part of her miserable destiny that the money ran out during the four years of Mr. Amor's illness, when her son was a small child, that she had to make artificial flowers to earn a living and do all the nursing single-handed. "I learned to care for him," she says, meaning to love him. Their marriage lasted for fifteen years.

If Beth walked unwittingly into traps it is because she is a romantic. "I *am* a romantic," she says. "I can cry about romance." Good looks would make her starry-eyed, as in the case of the sinister Harold; so, too, would the elegant use of the English language. The gambler mesmerized her with his beautiful letters. "You'd agree with me that his English grammar was so perfect." She fell in love with his letters, "the feeling that you have to have somebody to look up to and learn from." (The French language, brilliantly used, has had the same effect on me.) How could Beth know that this gracefully articulate man harboured an addiction, or that Harold's eyes, "so nice and clear," would turn cloudy? Too often, Beth's men, instead of being a way out, turned out to be a way in, into much more deadly poverty, or into real danger.

Beth's long walk on stones began not in childhood but with her first marriage. She didn't know that her family was "*very poor*," because "nobody seemed to have more than we did." "You must have eaten lots of oranges and milk as a child," said her dentist in Canada when he looked at her perfect teeth. "Well, no, we had a pint of milk a day and an orange around Christmas time." During the war, with no job and inadequate rations, she and her family were hungry all the time. Sometimes the butcher would let them have a little dripping "and you'd render that, beef drippings." But Beth isn't trying to win my sympathy, she's telling me how it is to start out poor, to go to work at fourteen in a cigarette factory (it was the best way for a girl to make money in those days), and to make people envious with your quickness. Whatever she tried, she did well, and I believe this, for I've seen the quickness coiled in her like a spring, as accurate as a heron spearing a fish. Snip, snip—she cut the end of an unfinished cigarette cleanly, without ever touching the paper, then snipped the other end as the belt doubled back. She was a "cutter" and then a "maker," she was "very very fast," earning more money than her father earned at cabinetmaking. "My goodness I was praised all the time," she says, for she even outwitted the floor lady, a wicked stepsister, who would furtively spoil Beth's finished cigarettes by snapping them in two. In life she has been more a doer than a maker, for she didn't deliberately choose her life but was borne along and flung about on its currents, the victim of forces much more powerful than she was. And yet she has a mighty will to survive; I could feel it out there in her concentrated stillness, beaming her will in this direction and that. Lost in thought, she seemed, until the word *Beth* was pronounced and she seemed to be startled out of a deep sleep, which was, in fact, total consciousness of everything and everybody around her.

I remember one day at the lake—heat, calm, waiting and the slight sounds in the distance of a scene in progress. Beth is sitting in the sun, I behind her in the shade with my hat over my eyes. A yellow swallowtail butterfly hovers over her foot, lands, lazily opens and closes its wings. "Beautiful butterfly," says Beth. "Stay here, little butterfly, stay with me. Oh! It flew away!" She plays this scene with dreamy artlessness, for no one except herself and the butterfly, it seems ("I thought you were asleep," she tells me), and I think, perhaps this is how she has survived; her sense of herself always at the centre of a drama has kept her alive through tragedy and privation. In another life, with more opportunity, she might have been a professional actress, she might have realized the dream that burns in her to be acclaimed as the *just me* that could fill a theatre with thunderous applause. Instead, there were jobs she always did exceedingly well, which sharpened qualities survivors need, but never fulfilled her longing to dazzle. Not until the film. "The film was the best thing in my life," she says. "I *loved* it, the excitement of it." And for the duration of the film, the things that had mattered ceased to matter and she lived her lifelong dream. Would she do it again? I wouldn't, I said. Of course she would.

L I N K

Our film is a semi-documentary. We are ourselves, up to a point; beyond this point is the "semi," a region with boundaries that become more or less imprecise, according to our view of them. In one sense, it is semi from beginning to end, for we wouldn't be out there in the wilds, wouldn't have boarded the bus together. Semi has worked to put together seven old women and a young woman who would never have known of each other's existence, with the ironic outcome that both in real life and on film we become friends who now need to keep in touch with one another. A real documentary might not have had this effect; it might have isolated each of us in her own life and surroundings. Out there on the three locations, links between us are forged in every scene. Consider two scenes from the shooting schedule, July 4th through 8th:

    #64: Tosses pills (Constance)

#69: Fishing with rocks (Cissy, Mary, Beth)

Both nutshell scenes contain a kernel of intractability by one of us: we balk at crossing the border into the semi. In #64, Constance is supposed to feel so rejuvenated by the sight of her childhood "water-house," as she calls it, and by memories of happiness there that she impetuously tosses her pills into the lake. "But I wouldn't do that," she says. "I'd be afraid I might need them." I, too, knew that even if I felt rejuvenated, I wouldn't throw away my pills. Old people cling to their pills. "Constance, just go ahead and do it, please," says Cynthia. "We can decide later." Later, in the cutting-room where our fate is determined.

"I hope you'll finish your snake," says Cynthia to Winnie at breakfast, "and then we can have the scene where you stuff it with grass." Winnie is knitting away on one of her brightly striped woollen snakes, which she stuffs with cotton batting. "Oh, I can't do *that*," she says, for even in fantasyland she won't stuff one of her snakes with grass. The art of snake-making has its rules. We all have rules, though we don't know what they are until we are asked to transgress them. Take *Fishing with Rocks* (Cissy, Mary, Beth), a good example of mildly indigestible semi. The three of us are standing at the edge of the calm lake, our feet planted well apart so that we won't topple into the water when we heave our rocks, which we hold in readiness. Looking down we see very small fish swimming in our shadows. "And—camera!" cries Cynthia, the signal for us to shout in unison, "One, two, three!" The waves made by our rocks ripple right up to our toes. With absurd solemnity we peer into the ruffled water. "It didn't work," I say gloomily. We do the scene over three or four times in a conspiracy of pretence. Personally, I'm ashamed of being caught doing something so dumb. "We'll have pâté of trout," I say, and we laugh.

"But I'd *never* wear anything like that." This is Catherine pronouncing judgement on the baggy grey cardigan that has been judged suitable for a nun, though her personal choice would have been closer to the plumage of a South American macaw. The distinctions we make between real and semi, between what we will and won't do, like or don't like, are perfectly clear to us. We are asked one by one, how do you feel about walking nude into the lake? That's how I understood the question, though Cynthia tells me that it was hedged with delicate precautions, which, in my panic, I didn't even wait to hear. My horror of the idea must go back to the irreversible prudery that was instilled in me seventy years ago. I reason with myself; I think of a painter friend, older than I am. In a documentary about her life, she walks naked down a beach and plunges into the sea. How I envy her freedom!

There are other no's in the domain of our dignity as old bodies, unworthy (some of us think) of display. Our vanity, too, is a factor, and the interiorization of supposed reactions an audience might have. "Grotesque, ridiculous, they're trying to make a laughingstock of us," says Constance about our splashing scene; she is looking through the eyes of a hostile audience. But the camera keeps rolling while we (Cissy, Alice and I) become ourselves as little children and, fully clothed, chase each other into the dazzling lake, scooping up warm water as we go. Alice goes in up to her waist, heaves gallons of water at Cissy and me; Cissy and I shriek in mock terror.

This scene, which gave us such joy and embarrassed Constance, vanished, and then reappeared in the final version. There were delicate feelings of rightness and wrongness to be considered in the cutting process, a sure instinct that spotted whatever was sentimental, over the top, inappropriate, boring. Not always agreement, of course: viewing the rushes over a thousand times, they would take something out or stick it back in again. Meanwhile, Constance's dismay, which weighed so heavily with her, made her repeat the words grotesque, ridiculous, we have nothing left but our dignity—to anyone who would listen. "Don't you agree? No, I see you don't," for I was answering her "everybody will laugh at us" with "they'll laugh *with* us."

How could they laugh, except with us, at our joie de vivre? I doubt if Constance's dismay weighed heavily in the decision to cut. Since we didn't know the criteria, we were the worst judges of what worked and what didn't work. We were being trimmed and shaped out of thirty hours of filming, reduced from miles of film to inches. Now and then the editors must have been startled by an audible squeak when their scissors cut through one of our cherished scenes, those scenes that still have a ghostly presence in our minds.

During the filming, however, there are times when one of us wants a scene cut—this, too, from a sense of what is appropriate, of which each of us is a judge. Thus Catherine, who somehow gets wind of the bootjack scene and learns enough about it to feel outraged. The scene consists of the demonstration in the house of a cast-iron bootjack in the shape of a buxom woman with legs spread, supposedly found in the barn. In reality, Gloria had found it in an airport boutique, and had been intrigued by its inherent violence as a sexist artifact. Something for the film, she must have thought. To pull off a boot you have to put one foot on the woman's face and the booted heel of the other between her legs and give a quick jerk upwards and backwards.

Winnie, Cissy, Alice and I are examining the thing. What can it be? they ask. I say it's a piece of nineteenth-century pornography and explain indignantly how it's used (Gloria has told me) and we try it with Winnie's foot shod in its little yellow shoe. All of us are surprised when it works to perfection. "Ow!" cries Cissy, "what a thrill!" "Oh, Cissy, you're impossible," I say. Afterwards, Catherine draws each of us aside and gives each the same piece of her mind. What is the scene doing there? It's demeaning, it's gratuitous feminist propaganda (this is like a dagger in my heart), it does violence to the spirit of the film. And, even in the heat of battle, I begin to think perhaps she's right. What is it doing? Isn't it the only strong dose of feminism in the film? Moreover, in the scene, I've worked myself up to a pitch of indignation (am I grotesque? Ridiculous?). I begin to be glad that Cissy laughed, with her laughter like a delighted child's. She hasn't seen the point, out there in that place that seems remote from boots on faces, boots jammed between women's legs. Can I legitimately use a piece of cast-iron in the shape of a woman as a pretext for a little lecture? Though they all look shocked by the way this old piece of cast-iron is put to use, and Alice says, "That's not right," none of them want to share my anger; it embarrasses them (I say to myself).

A few days later Gloria, having seen the rushes, says, "You'll be glad to hear that the bootjack scene has been taken out." A week later it is in again. And it is still in when we are shown the finished film, though the feminist message has appeared and disappeared. The same happens with many of the scenes that have had special import for us. In the cutting process they have become glancing and light-filled like fragments of a mirror flashing in the sun. They become very small facets of the whole, each with an identical importance, or elements of the composition that are held on the picture-plane by their place in the whole. So it's painting they've been doing, I think, or it's music. I begin to understand the editors' responsibility to eliminate negative or dead space. A scene that is even a minute too long becomes dead space; in this space a spectator has room to writhe with boredom or impatience. If the space is thought of as music, it may contain the right to linger in an adagio passage—say, the flight of a night heron across the evening sky. The heron is allowed to fly from east to west, and her leisurely beating wings carry messages about life and death and the meaning of the film. Her flight corresponds to the adagio scenes in which we talk about our fears. Birds and landscape in the film bear a burden of explanation that is as light as air: the heron's flight, the song of the white-throated sparrow, the early morning mist illuminated by pink sunlight. Now and then they serve as the expression of our hopes and fears; the cry of a bird is a synonym for Beth's terror of night in the country, and the song of the white-throated sparrow, which Constance can no longer hear, a synonym for the losses of old age. It is singing close by; she listens and does not hear it. "They used to be everywhere," she says.

W I N N I E

"They've got me yacking with Alice about my life. I'm not
going to tell them any secrets!" Winnie says. "Un-hunh-hah!"
Her little song, which in this case puts a seal on her secrets, often
comes out of the blue as if in answer to her thoughts. She agrees,
however, to come and tell me the main events of her life; my
doorbell chimes three times—Winnie's ring, jaunty like the
very small person (five feet, she says, and shrinking) I see at the
door, wearing a bright scarf under a big fur hat, and a beaver
coat down to her ankles. Touches of red: scarlet lipstick, scarlet
wrist warmers. And she moves as though, at 78, nothing creaks
or aches. "Hello, love," she says. So we begin the interview.
"Tell me about your life. Your mother? Your father?" Her
mother was a barmaid, didn't have much time for the daughters,
Stella and Winnie, who were "palmed off" to some people
named Holden and known as the "Holden chicks." "Your

father?" The man they *thought* was their father died when they were little. Their real father was "Uncle Joe," who lived nearby and was "married to a dame who was really a bitch—excuse the expression." "What was your name when you were born?" I ask. "I don't know. I'll have to look on my birth certificate. I think it was Holden. Don't bother to make sense of it," she says a little anxiously.

Stella was fourteen months older than Winnie and when she died in 1986, Winnie lost her dearest friend and life lost its meaning. "Once when we were little," says Winnie, "I got a hammerlock on Stella and tried to throw her out the window." I remembered the violent fights between my twin sister and me and laughed. When Winnie was eight years old, she and Stella walked four miles to and from school; no wonder she seems to skim over the ground. They were lucky if Uncle Joe gave them sixpence each to go to the movies, and supremely happy when a friend of their mother's brought them a chocolate cake with candied violets on it. You could get a meat and potato pie then for tuppence but tuppence was hard to come by. When Winnie was twelve she was still walking those eight miles to and from school, and she and Stella were doing the cooking, too. She tells me about her first paid job at fourteen, how she'd walk to the bus, take the bus to the ferry, cross the Mersey to Liverpool, take another bus to the cigarette factory, work there from eight a.m. to six p.m. with an hour off for lunch and make the same long trip in reverse. "It sounds like Dickens," I say. "Dickens. Yeah." At the cigarette factory the smell was "horrendous"; she describes her job: "chop, chop, chop, chop," for nine hours.

Winnie wanted to go into teaching, and what a wonderful teacher she would have made! For she's a born mime and a clown and can whistle exactly like a bird. The kids would have laughed all day long. And she would have taught them to love words and their meanings, for she can do the hardest crossword puzzles in the twinkling of an eye. Instead of which she has worked at thankless jobs without job security, a dismal series of them: she has worked as a parlourmaid (that was the worst, she says), mended china, taken care of a three-year-old kid, been a bus girl and then a waitress at Eaton's, worked in a typing pool, and so on. The job at Eaton's was "one of the better ones," since you got breakfast and lunch, and if you were lucky, could make a dollar a week on tips. Her salary was nine dollars a week, her room cost $3.50, you could get a meal for twenty-five cents, and she cleaned her clothes with kerosene and hung them on the roof. Somehow after three years she had cleared $1000 and could go back to England.

Stella and their mother had come to Canada, too, in 1931 in the middle of the great depression. An Englishwoman could pay £2 if she agreed to work in service for a year; if she paid £10 she could choose a job. All three got jobs right away: the mother as a housekeeper in Upper Westmount, Stella as a waitress, Winnie with the three-year-old kid. It was a time when "everybody" in Montreal spoke English, when "nobody" at Eaton's spoke French, when the stereotype of the "maudit anglais" was correct. Meantime Winnie was having a "very unhappy affair with an Italian guy from McGill studying to be a doctor. He couldn't marry me because his parents would raise hell." Roman Catholics? Yes. So he went back to the U.S.A. and Winnie went back to England and got a job as a dictaphone typist "for the gigolos" in a dance palace. Somehow during those dreary years she had learned how to type. "What was it like in Birmingham during the war?" "We were lucky really," says Winnie. Lucky not to be dead, that is. Lucky not to be in the next street or the next garden or "two doors up from where we were living when the bomb shelter with two kids and two women in it was blown up by a direct hit, and all we got was a cracked window." She went down with her mother to the official bomb shelter "in the middle of a sort of greensward, and you know, they had sackcloth drapes and pails for kids to wee wee in—and the smell! So we decided that if we were going to die we'd die in our own beds."

Birmingham, London, Liverpool—Winnie was in all of them and they were all hellish. You could see the flames in Liverpool from the Isle of Man. And then she joined the Wrens (the Navy), crossed to Gibraltar on an aircraft carrier, went through a storm in the Bay of Biscay, the proverbial place of storms. The Wrens were supposed to work in the fo'c'sle on typewriters slung in little hammocks. "I said no way!" And the table tipped over at supper and all the food was on the floor (she laughs), "It was a mess and cockroaches running around, you know." Several ships in their convoy were sunk that time. But they got to Gibraltar and it was heaven. The weather was glorious, the orange trees were covered with oranges, the Barbary apes looked in the windows at you. There were eighteen Wrens and 2400 men; "a lot of them committed suicide because there were no women and they were bored silly." "Weren't you besieged by men?" "Oh yeah," says Winnie. "I got engaged." But her man went off to Italy and stopped writing after a while. She has written me a postscript to the Gibraltar tale, headed *A Little Incident*, about an officers' party at which an officer filled up her glass with pure gin (she'd asked for water), "knocked me for a loop!" Then he offered me £200 if I would sleep with him!" A fortune back then. Befuddled as she was, Winnie had the presence of mind to refuse, and was shepherded back to the "Wrennery" by her friends. Gibraltar was mostly a lark, it seems, with dances and a trip to Algeciras, where the men found plenty of eager girls. (Spain was Fascist but this outing was permitted—one of those neutral safety vales that are part of the madness of war.)

She was demobbed on Christmas Day in 1945; went to Germany for a year with the Control Commission ("unh-hunh"), in transport, in the typing pool at £5 a week and "got so *bored*. So I thought, I'll never do another good day's work in my life if I stay *here*"—and went back to England. But fate had worked out her future; she was to come back to Canada (her mother and Stella were here) and become a citizen. "There was a place across the street where they sold canaries," she says. The Justice of the Peace was in the same building. "I just went over there, swore on the Bible and that was it." "Un-hunh, and now you have to go through a whole rigmarole." That was thirty-four years ago.

And life kept giving her a hard time. She lived with a friend in Verdun who kept the heat turned off, used to turn on the oven and put her feet in it, wouldn't help pay for the food . . . "un-hunh, it was a mess." She worked for CN telegraph, she went to Ottawa and worked at some kind of press job in Parliament. When? "I get these memory blanks . . . '54? 18 1/2 years, 8 1/2, oh 18 1/2, 19, 27, retired 12, 39, take 39, take 40, oh God," she laughs. Her mother had a sore toe; it was diabetes and they amputated a leg, and Winnie took care of her in her big old apartment over the Westmount paper store. The carpets were taken up, the doors were taken off; her mother fell out of her wheelchair and Winnie strained her back helping her up. It was too much for her so she put her mother in a nursing home where she was so doped up that she fell asleep over her meals. She said, "I want to come home, dear, give me my coat." And Winnie suffered for her mother in this awful place where the nurses were heartless and negligent, and where her mother died, three weeks before Winnie retired. "Then I retired, and there was nothing after fifty-one years of working," she says.

She took one more job, 11:30 to 7. "Time would go so slowly. So after three weeks I said who needs this? So I quit, and then I found this Senior Centre in Westmount and I've been happy ever since; it's like a second home." It made even her eviction notice more bearable, though she had been there for thirty-four years in the midst of her lars and penates. It was a big nineteenth-century apartment, with high ceilings, elaborate moldings and fireplaces, crumbling a bit around the edges. There were oil paintings by Winnie on the walls, macramé, weaving and stained glass by Stella ("she tried everything. You name it"), dolls, porcelain figurines and animals, a guitar, a huge sombrero.

She gave a lot of her treasures away (she gave me her portrait of Susie, Stella's white Pekingese) and drastically reduced the rest of her belongings to fit into her new apartment. The old one was the house of her soul, a domestic and creative soul, she had grown old in it, but she transported the important elements of it to the new place, which looks out at the great speckled tapestry of Westmount creeping up the mountain, pepper and salt in winter and tufty green in summer. And now she swims in the pool upstairs, takes an aerobic exercise class, walks briskly in every direction, but mostly east on de Maisonneuve to her Senior Centre, where she spends her happiest hours.

"I may look stoic," Winnie said to Gloria before the film was made, "but I'm not." Not stoic, I think, but what other word is there for her kind of uncomplaining fortitude? Patient, long-suffering, enduring—these are some of the synonyms for stoical. Enduring, but with her special Winnie-jauntiness. She never asks for sympathy or pity. Some of this is the British code of honour, I suppose; you bear whatever punishment you get and don't show that it hurts. The three Englishwomen in the film tell about the worst things in their lives with total objectivity, as though it were normal to have V-2 bombs whistling overhead (all three of them went through this), or a man with strange eyes put his hands around your neck (Beth), or to put in a fifteen-hour day at the age of fourteen. Winnie tells about the hell in her life in a matter-of-fact way—"un-hunh." The un-hunh this time is a form of reassurance, an affirmation of something going on in her head. My impression of the self inside the Winnie who has trained herself not to show emotion is of a person who will never ask for love, has suffered and will carry her old love-hurt in her forever, and will forever mourn the death of her sister Stella, her best friend. She is proud and sensitive, probably a bundle of nerves. She smokes; to Constance's "We'd be cranky," she said that to go three days without cigarettes—*that* would have made her cranky, with an emphatic un-hunh.

For fifty-one years of her life Winnie has slogged along from one awful job to another, she who could only give part-time (she painted, she played the recorder, she did weaving) to her gifts and never had the means to let them flourish. She has such a small collection of happy memories: one of them is the chocolate cake with candied violets on it, and paradoxically, life on the great rock, Gibraltar: sunshine and orange trees (but they cut down the orange trees growing near her barracks to put up Quonset huts), camaraderie and giddy times. And then the return to the grimness of postwar England and the pain of withdrawal from the Gib life of friends and perpetual sunshine. There were to be no more oases like that until she found her "second home" with the seniors in Westmount, and lived the long summer holiday of the film.

And now Winnie has a third home in her apartment building, a new life, new friends, parties in people's rooms, swimming, exercise in the gym. Two tenants have died since she came; two new tenants have moved in. Winnie helps friends in distress, tells me how her friend on the fourteenth floor (where the wind moans around the window) slipped on the icy street on New Year's Eve, fell and broke two ribs and a wrist bone. Winnie went to the hospital to visit her and brings her things to eat. "I'm happier here than I was on Sherbrooke Street!" she tells me. Unexpectedly, for I think she dreaded the move from the long-familiar to the unknown. In her second home I've seen her, wearing her scarlet vest, presiding over the game of chance, deadpan, witty, and I felt the kind of gladness you feel when you see a cardinal in mid-winter. She is one of a kind. Sui generis. And now she gives life to the impersonal apartment, speeds down its corridors, up and down in its elevators, a spark of bright colour like her scarlet vest. "O.K. love. See you later, love," she will say. She has created her own happiness out of her curiosity about people, her wit and courage. She's her own boss now, she says. She may say, "Getting old is the pits," but she's not going to let that spoil her new homemade life.

Postscript, April 13, 1990: Winnie reads these pages, laughs from time to time, tries to straighten out some facts ("Not 'chop, chop, chop': I pasted labels on cigarette boxes. Over fifty a day, you got a bonus") and dates. I said 1952, 1953, it didn't matter. *Does* it matter? That I've squeezed Winnie's long life into six pages and mixed up some of the transatlantic crossings of Winnie, Stella, and their mother? Stella was already here when Winnie came with their mother, she says. She'd forgotten to tell me something important: "my life wasn't that dreary," she says. There have been chinks of light in it through which sunshine poured, trips, tours. "I've been to Jamaica and Bermuda and Barbados and Puerto Rico and the Virgin Islands and Spain and Portugal and Texas and California and Mexico and Norway and Denmark." All these countries and islands are like the points of dazzling light one sees, lying in the sun with a tight-woven straw hat over one's face. Winnie wants to shift my attention, from the shadow cast by the hat to the bright sky beaming through minuscule holes.

I N T E R V A L

Dream (June 10, 1988): My doorbell rings; I open the door. My cleaning woman, her two daughters and her mother are there, all sobbing uncontrollably. The mother is curled up on a bed. She says, "Take me in your arms." She is old, skinny, almost toothless. I embrace her tenderly with my face close to hers. She is myself, I decide when I wake up, and I'm instructing the dreamer to be kind to herself (myself) as an old woman. It turns out that the film has the same message: be kind to yourselves as old women and to each other. Or do we give *it* the message by responding to the directors' apparent belief that we are only semi-old (they don't like the term "old women")? So it moves in a benign circle: to be thought of as semi-old, to feel semi-old, even to behave at times (too much, Constance thinks) like semi-children. The cameras, too, are in on the conspiracy, though we wear no make-up. Once we have lost our fear of their big eyes, we trust them to see us, not *exactly* like ourselves, but the way we feel. We begin to feel almost friendly toward them without knowing what they're up to, for when they seem to be at a safe distance, what they see may be only a few centimetres away. Just as well as that we aren't allowed to see any of the rushes!

We were semi-old. It was a lovely illusion that got us through long days without falling in our traces like decrepit cart-horses. It was the reason for our refusal to be in a nude scene, for wouldn't this have proved that we weren't semi but *old*? Young bodies should be celebrated and old bodies derided, according to society's dictum, proclaimed in books, films, advertising, television. We did not mind being filmed behaving like children in the splashing scene, but wanted our bodies to stay hidden in semi-reality, protected by clothes from the camera's (and cameraman's) eye. But, amendment on February 10, 1990: "No, no, no," says Cynthia, "it wouldn't have been that way." Not the way I feared, walking into the water naked with the usual male crew members on hand. We were to walk into the water wearing our bathing suits; a camera *woman* was to film us with our backs to her, after we had dropped our suits into the water. The set to be cleared; no men, that meant. But weather didn't permit and the lake got too cold. The seven of us in the calm lake with our backs turned—that was Cynthia's vision. So now, in the present, I telephone Winnie. She says yes, she'd understood all that but what would be the point of showing our old bodies? "Cynthia says we're *not old*," I say. "But we *are* old," says Winnie. "I'm 79, Cissy is 76," and so on to Catherine, the youngest of us, still in her sixties. Catherine, given all those conditions, might have been willing, says Cynthia. She mourns again, imagining her beautiful scene of our backs. She has to believe what she says—"But you're *not old*!"—since she knows and I know that it would have been a beautiful scene. "Backs stay young," she says. I'm secretly glad that the matter was settled by the impersonal decision of the weather.

Younger people can't tell us that we aren't old; we know better. Is my body the shapely one I see in this photograph of a young woman sitting on the edge of a swimming pool forty years ago? Far from it. What's more, I don't know when the process of irrefutable aging began; I didn't notice until it was too late. The screws of old age turn so slyly that it takes you by surprise. We stick with an interior image, the young woman sitting at the edge of the pool, even when her hair turns grey, then white. We select the photographs of us that make us look young, and hide or tear up the others. "Do I look like that? You've made me look so old," said Constance about the watercolour I did of her. "Am I so old?" asks a wrinkled Masai warrior I saw on television, looking at himself in a mirror for the first time, with a puzzled smile.

When we see the film, we suffer the same shock as the Masai warrior. So that's the way I look! "That dreary old woman," says Constance. For the first time in our lives we are separated from our mirror-images, the ones we can control, and have become Others. I see a tall woman dressed in pink and white, a little bowed, with a lined face, a toothy smile, hair as white as new-fallen snow. To the others, evidently, she looks just like me, as they look like themselves to me. And aren't our images of others more stable than those we make, from secondhand evidence, of ourselves? It must be so, for there are friends I haven't seen for twenty years who look at me and say, "You haven't changed at all." Is this because a pattern-face, the one that makes us recognizable, has swum up and taken over? Unless one has changed beyond recognition, this pattern-face will be superimposed on an older face, wrinkles, crepey neck and all, a kind of mask with the power (as Proust points out) to make old friends look as though they've been made up for a much older role. It only takes a few minutes for the face from twenty years ago to sink below the new one, to show through in familiar features: scrunched-up eyes, an assertive chin. The young person then has a new life in the old person, even if the old person is bent double with arthritis or has put on fifty pounds.

Childhood photographs, however, are merciless, and state the passing of time with inarguable clarity. We dig them out of our archives, learn how we were as children, as young women, and too often we do not recognize each other. I ache with the pain of seeing what we were long ago, when every one of us was beautiful with the beauty of a child or a young person full of careless energy. But if I study them at length, each merges mysteriously with the present friend in full colour, as Beth has merged, for the child and the young woman are both undeniably the Beth we know. And Cissy's round, puckered face forty years ago, can only belong to Cissy. And Catherine? Long before her vocation changed the shape of her life, she looked as she often looks now, like a grinning tomboy free as a bird. But we have all entered the cage of time and have been changed by the lives we haven't lived and by the one life we have lived. The unlived lives are conspicuous in the childhood photographs. Is this little blond angel (Constance) strong enough to contain her future? I see 88 years (90 now) and a big slice of Québec history packed into a body no bigger than a microchip; a long life, intelligence, beauty, energy, all are there, and the rest will fill up the minute spaces, and the little angel will turn into a poised young woman who looks familiar to us. Of all of us, Constance hates most being perceived as old, and recoils from her mirror-image. She tells me about the stranger riding beside her on a department store escalator, a well-dressed, attractive woman who looked like her and to whom she turned at the ground floor. She felt that she knew her and wanted to greet her. The woman had vanished; she was Constance's mirror-image. Constance realized with surprise that her mirror-image could please her as long as she was a stranger.

Out on the set, except for the fact that there is always someone to catch us if we stumble, or someone to set up folding chairs for us between scenes, we are beneficiaries of the semi which denies the passing of clock-time. There is nothing to remind us that we are old except direct comparison with all those staff and crew members who are young. In the outside world an old person is, all too often, either invisible to a young person or perceived as an obstacle or a doddering idiot. On location we are the centre of attention; all that paraphernalia is dragged around, set up, the sun is made to shine or the rain to rain, in order to make a beautiful picture of *us*. We can bask in a whole summer of attention, we are acting out the myth of our ideal selves, off- and on-camera, and we come to believe in our new reincarnations, there in the centre where the perspective lines meet. It doesn't matter that we, flesh and blood old people, are being translated into a film-language that expresses old people (us seven, at least) to Cynthia, Sally, Gloria and the others. They evidently want to show that old women don't necessarily dodder, quaver and shuffle. The attention so soothing to our egos, even if we know that it is the impersonal attention necessary to all filmmaking, is an exercise of their group will; all of the people standing and watching us are willing us into our semi-selves, until our image of how we'd like to be coincides with theirs. But we don't even fight; we don't say mean things about each other, we are, by and large, our best selves. I took my best self back to Montreal with me and was surprised when she was displaced by the old self, subject to the usual fits of crankiness. Almost as if the old self said to the best self, "Who do you think you are? I'm still here." Like an old cat growling at a new kitten.

In the first rushes, Sally says, we seemed (as we were) almost strangers to each other. Our becoming friends off the set changed the nature of the film and made scenes of discord or violence impossible. Or a death scene. Any kind of pretence, and above all, a pretended death, would be false to the spirit of the film. But before this process began, of our helping to determine the direction of the film, Gloria had written a scene in which Constance dies. "Constance: Not asleep," she wrote.

An evasion? Even then Gloria felt the danger in the words for the end of life: dies, death, dead, could not spell them out, could not fix the spell on one of us.

During the entire filming we are invisible to ourselves, but each must have had a private image different from the one we see when we are shown the film. How strange she is, I think of the Mary I see; she has a slow, creaky voice and a face like her mother's crackleware teapot. Because we are sealed into our bodies, we are surprised by things in ourselves that we have never noticed and that now seem exaggerated and slightly embarrassing. We are seeing new selves—the real ones? or the ones that others see? It must be this, for the others don't seem strange to us, as each of us is strange to herself. Constance and I feel a little guilty; we've been pretending to be something we're not, i.e. younger, and now the secret is out. The camera doesn't lie. But the second time Constance and I see the film we are less embarrassed by these other selves; we almost like them. Constance still grumbles about herself, to be sure, but with a hint of reconciliation. A kind of focussing is going on, a lining up of self- and film-images. We have to learn to let go of all our preconceived ideas, both about how we look and about the nature of the film. "Nothing happens," says Winnie. I tell her that *we* are what happens. The film is about seven semi-old women and a young woman happening.

Constance begins to doubt the existence of the film. "They've let it go," she says. Mirage-like, it moves away from us; it will be shown this fall, next year, in January, April, or June. Our fragile film is lost somewhere in the entrails of the Film Board—how can it possibly survive peristalsis, "the peculiar wormlike wave motion of the intestines . . . forcing their contents onward"? (Webster) It is moving, Cynthia tells us in November at Constance's party, for we gather together now and then for proof that most of us are still alive, still fond of each other. (But Gloria is dead, Cissy is fading away in a rest home and Catherine has moved to California.) "The editing is all done," says Cynthia, and we take heart again.

"I've turned into a couch potato," said Winnie the other day. Out there we had a holiday from growing old; here we are moving along on a conveyor belt like luggage at an airport, see in front of us the place where the luggage passes through a curtain of plastic strips and disappears into darkness. Perhaps that's why Beth would like to do the film all over again, to get off the conveyor belt, step out of time. To be protected from time. "It's awful to grow old," says Constance with angry energy. How can young people understand how awful it is, she says, to have lost control of your body, which changes for the worse without permission? With stubborn courage, Constance cooks, gives parties, plays bridge, reads, discusses books with unfailing alertness. Cissy went on gardening until she was stopped by an aneurism. Beth and Winnie walk a lot and Winnie's schedule of activities would do me in. But "getting old is the pits," she says. She has had cataracts removed; so has Constance. I'm another couch potato, and dream about old age and death—dream-metaphors that are crystal clear. I want to get rid of my Toyota and get a Studebaker (I had one thirty years ago) or I run my car into a snowbank, can't go an inch farther. "It's not funny to be old and vulnerable," says Constance. She wears a beeper around her neck to summon help if she needs it. I think of her dream, of her standing at night in the empty street, waiting for a bus that does not come.

CONSTANCE

The filming is far behind us now but we (the cast) still see each other and talk to each other on the telephone. And one day Constance calls to tell me, "Something terrible has happened. I hear music in my head all the time. It's pure torture, I'm not myself. I'm depressed and sad. I think I'm going to die. I've just done a little ironing; I've made my lunch. Do you know what played all day yesterday? 'Nearer My God to Thee,' all day long. Today—great chords. It's not rock music or anything; it's pretty. It goes away when I turn on the radio." She keeps the radio on all night to drown out the music in her head. "Nearer My God to Thee," an old circuit reconnected, haunting her unbelief. It reminds her of her ecstatic belief when she was a child, a little convent girl, and mockingly offers her hope. The dead, too, have come to haunt her. "It's so funny, in my old age

I think of my mother." Her mother is present and Constance is "hantée par les regrets."

In *Recollections of a Québec Childhood*, Constance says that before her "impending arrival," the fifth child, hard on the heels of her nearest sibling, a letter of sympathy came from her paternal grandmother to her mother "with the sincere wish that God would interfere and take away the unwanted child. But the prayers remained unanswered. Not only was I born, but I was followed by four more children." Constance, "unwanted," indoctrinated in her mother's womb and born against her mother's wish, still carries her burden of original guilt. But she and her mother "weren't on the same wave length at all at all at all," she says. Her mother was a believer who looked forward to dying; God gave her the strength to get through the sorrows of her life. Her father took morphine to kill the pain of facial neuralgia and became addicted. Constance describes her father's sad face, his desperate eyes, his ransacking of the house when her mother tried to regulate his pills. In spite of this shadow over the family, Constance's childhood was happy. Her parents were Québecois who had moved to Fitchburg; her father, until his decline, was highly respected as a doctor. They lived in a big house, had servants, two horses and two carriages; on some great occasion in Boston Constance "was one of the babies," she says, "who sat on Theodore Roosevelt's knee."

When Constance was eight years old, the family moved to Chicoutimi to be under the wing of prosperous uncles and aunts. There she was one of a swarm of siblings and cousins and older relatives. If her Catholic aunts prayed all the time, believing that prayer would hasten her father's recovery, it didn't dampen her spirits. Her account of the year before she was sent to the Ursuline convent is full of the joys of winter, of summer, of sleigh rides, of great family gatherings, which laid the groundwork for her lifelong social ease and her love of life. As for the convent, where she was sent with three of her sisters, its mediaeval religious atmosphere was capable either of crushing the spirits of a child, or, in Constance's case, of filling her soul with exaltation. She and her sisters, who did not yet speak French, were plunged into strangeness: "among strange children, strange teachers, eating strange food and living through long days filled with strange occupations." The health and spirit of one of the sisters were permanently broken, but Constance was happy and thrived; in her state of innocent belief she accepted her new world "where sin and guilt dominated every thought and act." "They were obsessed by sin," she says to me on the telephone. "They talked of nothing else. And all these little girls believed every word of that nonsense." Constance was the brightest of them all; she had read dozens of books, she had artistic talent, she sang solos in the choir, she was the leading lady in every play ("Je faisais la Sainte Vierge, or whatever it was," she says). She loved the landscape around the convent, the great lake that stretched to the horizon, turned black in autumn, then white, then blue in spring and summer. She describes the bitter cold and the joyful coming of spring, with lilacs, buttercups, daisies, "beehives in a field of clover." (The bees spent the winter in the cellar under her dormitory and she could hear them buzzing.) Constance is as sensitive to landscape as any painter; indeed, our film-story grows out of her longing to see a lake and a little boat-house at the edge of it, which she had remembered from childhood.

"We got up at 4:45 a.m.," says Constance, "said a first prayer, washed (it was a very summary washing, I assure you), sat in chapel, half-awake while the nuns chanted, the priest said mass. I didn't suffer at all. I loved it." She loved God. At her first communion she had "thought of her soul as a small room, like a room in a doll's house, and God occupied it, sitting in a throne-like chair." Now she looks back, laughs drily, smiles her ironic smile for the child who believed everything she was told. "If God was displeased he became vengeful and cruel. He had not only created hell, but he created also human beings to throw into it. A guardian angel was ever-present to protect you from sin. This person was male, and it was necessary to be always modest because of his constant presence beside us." Inspired justifications for keeping people in order! The Protestants have no handsome guardian angel for enforcing modesty. At Constance's convent not a word could be uttered between seven p.m. and seven a.m.; this was called "le grand silence." How much more poetic this term is than the "communications rule" that forbade us, at my Protestant boarding school, to speak or even to exchange looks between classes or at bedtime. The Ursuline convent was peopled with ghostly presences, who either kept order (God, Jesus, the saints, the guardian angels) or disturbed it (the devil), and indefinable, unmentionable threats: sex and death. Death stole little children by the hundreds, decimated big families (one of Constance's aunts lost ten of her sixteen children), stalked the corridors of convents and went off with children and nuns. Constance's sister, Hectorine, died of tuberculosis at sixteen, joined "le cortège des vierges" and the company of youthful saints.

In her state of love, Constance lived within the iron cage of rules with its spying and punishment, accepted it all, including endless prayers on knees calloused from kneeling. The other pupils were for the most part farmers' daughters being trained to a life as pious farmers' wives. At the convent, pigs were slaughtered, vats were filled with blood, the little girls were taught how to make blood pudding, how to stuff "yards and yards of gut with sausage meat." They learned cooking, bee-keeping, spinning and weaving. "It was fun," she says.

But love got her into trouble, love embellished by make-believe. From the beginning, her fertile imagination had helped her to invent sins to feed to M. le Chaplain at confession: "I had lied. I had been greedy. I had said unkind things about others. I had been disobedient, proud, vain, lazy, envious." M. le Chaplain must have smiled to himself when he gave her absolution. True, she did sometimes lie, and stuck to her lie, when it was suspected, with amazing courage. A kind of lie was at the core of her trouble and her punishment. Mère Sainte-Marie, the blue-eyed, pink-cheeked nun she loved, gave her a "small holy picture," which she hid in the prayer book in her desk, after writing on the back, "A ma chère Constance, avec mon affection, Mère Sainte-Marie." The picture disappeared and Constance was called before la Mère Générale and made to kneel with outstretched arms. She confessed, but then—she giggled, one of those untimely giggles I, too, knew as a child, and la Mère Générale slapped her face. Constance would not be given the prize she deserved for best student, she said; she said, too, that Mère Sainte-Marie had been unjustly accused. Constance had seen Mère Sainte-Marie with red eyes; they never spoke again, and Constance crept around the convent like a wounded animal, unable to hide from her guilt.

Constance, who by magic had made her wish for love more real, was innocent except in the context of the spy system. La Mère Générale's obedience to rules prevented her from caring whether she ruined two lives; otherwise she would have left the holy picture in Constance's prayer book and kept quiet about it. The devil himself must have whispered into la Mère Générale's ear that God would approve severe punishment for a little girl who had committed forgery and then had the nerve to giggle about it. To this day, Constance asks herself, "*Did* I commit a grave offence? Was the punishment fair?" "I agreed that I didn't deserve the prize after what I'd done," she says in her *Recollections*. But the humiliation of it still burns.

May 3rd, 1990. A long telephone conversation with Constance. I ask her about Mère Sainte-Marie, whether her sin was to have given Constance the holy picture. No, says Constance, the nuns were permitted to give these pictures. Her sin was a suspected "amitié particulière" with Constance. "Of course I was in love with her," says Constance, "but there was no sex. The nuns were terrified by the remote suggestion of sex." She tells me that when they formed game-circles with the little girls they turned down their sleeves so as not to touch naked hands. "A layer of cotton," says Constance dreamily. She loved this: it added to the mystery of love. Even as a child, she loved veils. "The business of masturbation, orgasms," she continues. "The nuns were scared to death of the words." I say to Constance that I didn't know until I was grown up what the words masturbation and orgasm meant. "But you must have had orgasms when you were a child!"

Constance harks back repeatedly to the joyful time of belief at the convent. "I was extremely pious, I went to the chapel to pray, God was part of my life, communion was a real and thrilling thing." She misses her innocent, heartfelt faith, which made even hardship joyful, wishes that she hadn't lost it. It was a gradual disenchantment helped along by books; she says that H. G. Wells' *Outline of History* was one that dealt her faith a final blow. "It was very comforting, you know, to be able to go into a church and say a few Hail Marys," she says one day on the telephone. She tells me about her hairdresser, who says to God, "It's your affair. You just decide what you want to do with me." "I don't believe in God, do you?" says Constance. I say, no, I don't; I believe in eternity but get dizzy when I think about it. "All those people," says Constance, "with their prayer beads and their masses. They're thrilled because they're going to heaven. But you can't pretend. What seems to be the truth is that there's nothing at all, nothing at all." Alone in her apartment she contemplates nothingness and listens to the reproaches of the dead. She remembers how her sister waved to her from the window of her retirement home: "She saw my car drive away," says Constance mournfully; she had driven away to her own life. But now Constance has become her sister. "I'm deteriorating very fast," she says. "I walk with difficulty. Pretty soon I won't be able to walk any more." That same day she may make lunch for three friends and play bridge all afternoon, but the fear crowds back into her mind when she is alone again.

Constance heard the music in her head for several days:

"songs and noise, it's frightening. I wish we had something, somebody to cling to; I feel like a child that needs its mother—lost, abandoned. I feel frightened, I feel awful, I think about death all the time, every day." Finally the music stopped and she felt better. I think back to a conversation Constance and I once had, in which we talked about dying. "Are you afraid of dying?" she asked me, and I said, "Yes, I am." But the truth is that I don't know how afraid I am and won't know until I have to face my death. Constance, still so alive, has been facing her death, and knows more about the fear of death than I do. But on the set she said with her little laugh, her melodious, slightly drawling chuckle like the heh-heh of a seagull high overhead, "The script calls for somebody to die. I think it's going to be me." Out there she could think calmly, it's logical for me to be the one; I'm the oldest. I imagined Gloria playing with the temptation to have one of us die, stroking the edge of the thought as if it were a sharpened knife, and drawing back from the danger of it. It was dangerous even to think of the word "death," for we were playing ourselves, old people lost in the wilds. Constance took our plight literally and objected to our high spirits. "We wouldn't be happy, we wouldn't want to sing, we'd be tired and hungry and cranky." She raised her voice to say these words: *tired, hungry, cranky,* emphatically, meaning that she didn't want to be argued with. But to be chosen to die would be as frightening as dreaming one's own death; it was frightening even then that Gloria, whom death was seeking without her or any of us knowing it, had the power as writer to lay the spell on one of us. And didn't do it, for it is a film about life, about resisting death.

No, we could not die, either on- or off-camera. Off-camera, something out there protected us from the serious danger of our falls, bruises, high blood pressure, nausea, near sunstroke or exhaustion. Constance's bruises were as colourful as a sunrise: yellow, purple, blue, with red lacerations pricking through her almost transparent skin. She was squashed against the front door of the van when we tipped into the ditch, she fell against a sharp piece of furniture in the TV room, her blood pressure soared. The frail and wobbly structure of us, the underpinning of the film, was held together either by magic or by prayer peculiar to filmmakers: don't get sick! don't die! Wait! Out there, Constance, who now thinks constantly about death, was distracted by happiness, laughed almost with pride at her lurid bruises, won in battle. We stood between her and death; we surrounded her, as whales and dolphins surround one of their own and bear her up. Constance wasn't allowed to feel the anguish of solitude, and her death-thoughts were expressed tranquilly, as if to say, this is a subject as banal as the weather.

Constance is the same age as our century. She prefers to think that 1900 was the last year of the nineteenth century; she says that she doesn't belong to the twentieth. She was ten years old the year my parents were married, and might have been a flower girl at their wedding. She stands between them and me, belongs to their time and to my time; she insists that she is "an old fogey," and I say that anyone born before 1920, including me, is an old fogey. "I'm very fond of you," she says on the telephone, "I feel you filled a gap in my life." I tell her that I'm writing about her. "What have you got to say about this old, boring, depressed woman? I don't know how anybody can stand me. I'm so depressing. I'm critical, I'm mean. That's why my children don't like me." This is standard Constance. You praise her, show interest in her, say you like something she's wearing, and it starts pouring out as if you'd pushed a lever. I utter my usual protests, sometimes saying no, you're not, sometimes saying that I'm just as mean, just as critical. "Are you?" That cheers her up.

Next time we talk she tells me that Mme de Baudoin who shares her apartment has taken her for an evening outing. "She took me to Parc Lafontaine and we sat on a bench. There was a lovely soft breeze blowing. It was like going to a different country, everybody gay and happy." In spite of Constance's automatic response to any threat to her long habit of hating herself, which she wears next to her skin like a hair shirt, there is a wellspring of gaiety always ready to bubble up, the source of her life. It can be turned on by the sight of children or animals, by memories of our film, by sampling a perfect chocolate, by reading a good book, by good conversation, for she is above all a social being. Her dark self flourishes in loneliness and is rooted in the dead who haunt her, and in her fear of death. She tells me of a recurrent dream in which she is at the corner of Greene Avenue and Ste. Catherine as they looked before the big buildings went up. It's dark and she's waiting for a bus that doesn't come. She's entirely alone in the empty street and wakes up in fear and anguish. I tell her that it's a dream about loneliness and the fear of death and she is silent, frightened perhaps.

"I'm not a happy person," she says. "I've had nice parents, nice children, a good life, but I'm not happy." She quotes Borges' poem "The Brooder," about a man "born to be happy" who chooses instead to become a brooder. Constance frequently identifies in spirit with great writers (all men): Lorca, Proust and now Borges. In Ronda, Spain, she held the hand of a bronze statue of Lorca that stood in the stairwell of the hotel; at Combray she lay down, when the guardian was out of sight, on Proust's bed. Fortunately he did not see her committing this impious act but caught her with a sprig of lily-of-the-valley from the garden in her hand. "Madame," he said reproachfully, "je vous ai fait confiance." These were rites of holy communion with her gods. Now Constance partakes of Borges, who gives respectability to one of her few sins—to hate herself. While the film was being made we were the buffer zone protecting her against her despairing thoughts, old grievances, irreparable hurts and injustices. It is impossible to prevent her from setting traps to catch her self-esteem and then deliberately walking into them. She finds the most ingenious reasons for not liking either her film-self or the self she sees in the mirror. We saw her in the film as dignified and beautiful; she saw herself as "a dreary old woman, a killjoy." "I'm ugly, I'm fat. So that's the way I look." "I'm very disappointed," she said at the end of the showing, in a voice that rang like a knell in the silence. She wishes not to be convinced that she's wrong. She sets out to prove to herself that she is no longer young and beautiful by going out and buying a dress, a jacket, a hat or a skirt. She tries on the jacket for me to see, looks at herself in the mirror and hates her mirror image. "It makes me look too fat, don't you think?" I say no, it's perfect; she doesn't believe me. She falls into a state of depression and plans to return the jacket, over my objections. "I don't know why I have to think of myself as chic and svelte the way I was thirty years ago. It's vanity, I guess."

She was born to be happy; thirty, forty years ago there must have been times when the vibrancy of her body, her quick mind, her beauty (the beauty that is still there, whatever she may think) made her giddy with joy. Times when she was mistress of her soul, the six years, for instance, during and after World War II when her radio program on CBC stirred the whole of Canada. About this time she is still proud but can't resist belittling it: "I was nothing but a housewife, I felt it was ridiculous for someone like me to do it, a fool rushing in. I was a fool. I read everything I could get my hands on. I had an opinion, the only one, I'm told, who had an opinion [she laughs]. I imagined an ideal listener, a woman in the prairies, a housewife like me with a child sleeping in the next room." "What did you do with your radio speeches?" I asked her. "I threw them in the garbage." I groaned. I can hear her voice, as light as air but firm and musical, a hint of melancholy in it, a hint of her little laugh, an almost imperceptible drawl in the inflection. She could speak of portentous things with this voice. "I was the first to put the news of the hydrogen bomb on the air." I think of her voice flying like a bird's, carrying the unimaginable weight of the hydrogen bomb to the far reaches of Canada. She was the only reporter to have heard the news at dawn. I think of the small, exquisite young woman, bodiless, faceless for her listeners, her voice lightly bearing the news of the end of the world. Later: Cynthia digs a memory out of her childhood, of hearing Constance on the radio, of thinking excitedly: women can do something wonderful with their lives!

Constance's happiness is held in memories, in nostalgia. "Do you remember how it was with the sun shining on the lake?" Even the film, so close in time, is far away now, and a soft regret, as if for a beloved dead friend, creeps into her voice when she speaks of it. In the present, an incubus sits on her shoulder, whispering in her ear about old age and death. The past contains times of bliss—the birth of her first baby, exquisite, perfect (and all the mothers in the cast speak with the same wonder about this marvellous time before the baby grows up and takes its distance). The past contains the death of her favourite brother and of one of her daughters. I have seen a photograph of a boy sitting in a canoe on a calm lake, turned sideways, smiling, her brother who died young. Photographs of the living who will die tremble with their innocent, ignorant vitality. Constance's life has been full of sorrow not of her own making. And some of her making: her futile remorse, her feeling of being unloved. Constance believes that she is a sinner—the legacy of church-going long after you have stopped going to church. The bleakness of all those old warnings and scoldings haunts Constance's unbelief. Along with Borges' "The Brooder," she loves "The Waste Land," that poem of utter despair.

The fears that were planted in Constance as a child are still there; they put on different masks, take different shapes, all terrifying. She is still under the shadow of her father's drug addiction, of the silence and denial. But she can coax up lovely memories of Christmases, summer holidays, boyfriends, her early love for nature, "lakes, silence." At twenty-one, she married the man whose portrait by Jori Smith is hanging in the living room. (I stare at his bald head, his bon vivant's mouth, the sensual little smile that seems to recall a past pleasure.) "He was a kind man," says Constance. He died at 93 from a fall in the street. "I should have gone out with him," says Constance. "It wouldn't have happened."

Yes, according to society's standards Constance has had a good life. She uses this against herself, too, that she is a brooder in spite of her apparent good fortune. Personally, I think that this "good life" prevented some of her great talents from flourishing. Isn't this clear from her success as a broadcaster? "A small success," she demurs. She could have been the governor general; I can imagine her in her element at Rideau Hall, exercising all her charm and ease with people, her knowledge of Canadian politics, her bilingualism. She threw her speeches "in the garbage." Garbage is one of her recurrent themes, I realize. Has she ever seen Samuel Beckett's *Endgame*, in which a man and a woman are up to their necks in two garbage cans for the length of the play? "I have an idea they're going to throw it in the garbage," she says about the film. Or, "they've already thrown it in the garbage, haven't they?" And death does the same; you are disposed of "like garbage." Decay and disposal. Constance sees herself, isolated by her deafness, more and more alone until she is taken off to a nursing home (her greatest fear) to die. "What are we doing here?" she asks me. "I have the feeling that I won't last long." And adds with a little flare of humour, "I've had that feeling for years." We are both disgusted by the same things. I call her, she says about the film, "I hope it's not absurd and ridiculous." "But you liked it the second time!" I say. "Oh, did I?" And goes on to talk about Henri Troyat's biography of de Maupassant: "une histoire de prostituées et de bordels. This was what he preferred. He had syphilis. Troyat parle d'un monde dégoûtant, une personne dégoûtante." One by one the gods topple; they were all personnes dégoûtantes. Their lives should be thrown in the garbage and one's attention riveted to their work. Disgust wells up in some of us in old age, and begins in our own bodies, which are betraying us, we think, in disgusting ways. (Simone de Beauvoir felt disgust for her body when she was thirty-five.)

Constance, ma petite soeur ainée, unalike as we are, unalike as our lives have been, we share the bad things that bind people together or tear them apart: doubt, fear, guilt, disgust. Constance is much less squeamish than I am: in marriage, wives shed a lot of squeamishness. Now that Constance is husbandless, an "old, old party," as she says, she is like a charming, worldly-wise teenager, and this delightful person lives inside the other older one who looks at herself in the mirror with unreasonable dislike. I see her at the Château Borghese after a raid on their boutique, looking as though she has just eaten a particularly delicious chocolate. She is wearing a new white tam-o-shanter made of Icelandic wool, and a soft mohair sweater, striped grass-green and white. The little girl, Constance, is peeping out mischievously, and for once, with real pleasure. And then the older Constance, ever ready to snatch away her pleasure, says, "I should give it to my granddaughter, shouldn't I?"

"Comme le cristal vibre encore/ Longtemps après qu'on l'ait touché." This is the love song Constance has sung to us in her pure, frail voice. She is that crystal, still vibrating. She tells me that a few years ago she went back to visit her Ursuline convent and was recognized by a nun, old as the Biblical Sarah, who remembered, still carried the image of the little girl Constance and the sweet sound of her voice. A small miracle, the exchange of memories from old mind to old mind. "Now I'm an old old old party," says Constance on the telephone. "Well, stay as long as you can," I say. "I love this place. I love this world," says Constance.

S N A P S H O T

W I T H   A   D O G

A line-up: six of us (Catherine and Constance do not appear in this one) on the porch of the old house at Boileau. Beth, Cissy, Winnie are sitting on a big wooden box close to the green-shingled wall; I'm next; my left hand is touching the back of a shaggy white puppy, standing with one big paw in front of Alice's right toe. Alice, on a milk crate, appears to be perched over space against the bright blue sky, leaning over with her hands between her knees like Picasso's Gertrude Stein. Right foreground: a leg is sprawled out with a bandage wrapped around the ankle, another leg with knee raised, a white sock, a red shoe. These legs, in white pants, belong to Michelle. We are all wearing our costumes, pale colours that will coalesce in the film in a pastel composition that makes no statement about who we are or where we come from. We are looking thoughtfully, wonderingly down (each pair of hands arranged to suit the character) at the puppy, knee-high, with the paws, black eyes and nose of a young polar bear. The line-up contains its own present and an unimaginable future.

The dog will be named Molly; she will be Gloria's Molly, but in the line-up she has no name, is an orphan, found tied up in a garage by one of the crew. She has a pink flush along her spine and on her ears, she is wide in the hips, and is presumed to be some sort of terrier. Her pink tongue is bordered by the smiley loop of her upper lip; her ordeal is over, she has found love. We are all in luminous sunshine, but there is a blue shadow in the lower right-hand corner, lying over the toe of Michelle's red shoe and turning it purple: Gloria's shadow (she is taking the photograph). Gloria's future is in that small Prussian-blue shadow, which, for the moment, only has the power to turn the tip of a red shoe purple. And Molly? I name her and will become one of "Molly's aunts," committed to her welfare. For Gloria it is love at first sight. Molly has not yet betrayed the Old English sheepdog in her by the sudden little sneer that lifts her black lip and shows a threatening glimpse of snowy teeth; it goes with a defiant toss of the head, a prance of her big feet. She has no intention of obeying the command to lie down, and then, surprise—she collapses like a rag doll and falls asleep. Molly becomes one of Gloria's alter egos. In contrast to Alison, the bear hand-puppet, who expresses submission, shyness and a wish to please, Molly expresses Gloria's longing to abandon herself to riotous joy.

Shortly after the snapshot was taken, Molly was banished from the set. But even when she was invisible, the Molly-problem was there and grew along with her as she passed that summer from aunt to aunt or dragged Gloria around Parc Lafontaine, and filled up most of her little house. When Gloria got cancer, she still clung to Molly, so bouncy, so cheerfully smiling, who jumped up, almost capsizing Gloria in the process, and embraced her in a great white flurry of reassurance. The aunts all knew that Molly embodied Gloria's hope.

Molly spent her summer holiday in the country with me; she grows from photograph to photograph. In the first, a puppy with a blunt nose, still easily liftable by Gloria, who has come to visit her darling. By the end of the month Molly's back feet dangle almost to Gloria's knees, and Gloria's feet are spread to support the weight. Her head is tipped sideways, a smile of incredulous pleasure on her face. She photographs me photographing Molly, who is gazing at her reflection in the pond. Photographs in the present (I am looking at them), concentrated life. Gloria drives over from her father's house in Knowlton for a big draft of high spirits, with friends who know how to enjoy life, unlike her friend, Mary, who does not drink or smoke, who goes to bed at ten o'clock and boots people out of the house if they stay too long. Or tries to. Everybody, including Molly, agrees that I am hopelessly austere. It is hard, after they have consumed several bottles of wine, with Gloria now in her seventh heaven of jollity, to persuade her to go home. She sits sadly at the wheel of her Honda Civic, while Molly jumps up and begs her to stay. "Just five minutes longer?" Gloria begs like a child resisting bedtime. Pitiless friend, she must think about me, as she drives off into the night.

G L O R I A

During the whole summer of 1988, Gloria looked conspicuously well; her face glowed, her laugh rang out. She stood for most of the day in her special stance—feet and knees together, back straight. I teased her by saying that she looked like Smoky the Bear but she looked much more, I told her later, like an Egyptian "shabti," one of the round-faced spirits of the dead whose full bodies taper down to slender legs and small feet. The shabti stands with folded arms and "acts as a deputy of the deceased should any work be required of her in the Afterworld." The one I saw in the British Museum was the deputy of a singer priestess. I showed a postcard of her to Gloria when she was sick, and she looked at it intently for a long time. Even ten days before she died, her face was still round, bronzed by the sun; she looked like the Egyptian shabti. Her eyes were intensely dark and bright; they held her familiarity with the idea of her death.

The day Gloria came to my house with Cynthia, her being was rearranged, like iron filings rushing toward a magnet and clinging to it. I was the magnet, but I didn't know how fatally until the filming was underway and I felt Gloria's eyes on me in every scene. "It makes me self-conscious when you look at me so much," I plucked up the courage to say. Gloria's eyes, detached from her head, seemed to follow me even when she was sitting at her computer with her back turned, when I flew silently past her open door down the corridor of the Château Borghese. I wanted to go down to dinner by myself, to ally myself with my friends downstairs; I wanted to ease into my place between Edna and Alice, and greet the others who were already seated at the long table surveying the dinner menu. It was important to me to be with *them*, whereas to huddle with Gloria might somehow betray them. I might know in this way more than they did, might not want to tell them what I knew, and this could drive a wedge between us. Even if Gloria was the soul of discretion, only giving me, with her mischievous look, a tidbit scarcely bigger than a crumb (I had a sneaking longing to know about inner workings, rivalries, feuds, fits of temper), I didn't want to know *too much*. Too much might topple the carefully wrought structure in my mind, which preferred to make its own observations, even if they were wrong. And I was afraid of being perceived as a lesbian who is only comfortable in the company of another lesbian. Ordinarily, lesbians are eager to talk to each other and exchange tales of suffering or happiness, and Gloria was stocked with reminiscences (like Beth, she had "walked on stones") that might have lasted a lifetime of friendship and were to last only a little over a year. Yet she managed to tell me about the worst things, those that had almost wrecked her life. Stories of her own shipwrecks and how she crawled away from them.

The day I became the magnet for Gloria's attention, she saw me as the lesbian she had dreamed of for the film. She believed that wishes have magic power and that if you wish hard enough the wish will come true. And wasn't her wish to become part of my life, to weave me into the structure of the film, a magic wish, didn't I appear as a magical being who could bring her happiness? All the more magical because of the shipwrecks, the stony deserts she had traversed before the day when she and Cynthia rang my doorbell. I felt the pressure of her wish; a wish, a gaze are identical, both compelling attention. After much shilly-shallying, I wrote a letter refusing to be in the film at all. I would miss my summer of painting and writing, I said; I would be exhausted, and I didn't like the ambiguity of my role. Would I be in the film because I was a lesbian? Would I have to act the part of a lesbian? I could only be myself, I said. My letter, which seemed so reasonable to me, reduced Gloria to tears. "I was so happy to have a lesbian," she said, "Your not being in *The Bus* [the working title then] is like trying to paint a picture without red paint. The picture can't exist without that red paint." As it turned out, I was happy to be some brushstrokes of lavender paint, part of the whole composition, and not the swatch of red that Gloria had wished for. But Gloria's first wish came true; I became a piece of the structure of the film. And I became part of the time she had left to live. A friend. "Will you be my friend forever?" she asked suddenly, when she was sick. "Swear it with your blood."

"WE DON'T KNOW YET WHAT IS GOING TO HAPPEN ON DAY 3": this is announced at the bottom of a pink sheet of paper marked DAY 2, which Gloria had typed for distribution to the cast. The story, in sketchy form, is on pink paper; the scenes are numbered on blue paper. Gloria could look into the future and map our scenes without knowing either the order or context in which they'd finally appear. Or whether they would appear at all. DAY 3, the immediate unknown, now seems to stretch beyond the end of the film, to contain Cissy's damaged brain and

Gloria's sickness and death. DAY 3 was the area of the film, the area of life, that Gloria could not predict. In the film-DAY 3 we exercised our "reality," or our free will. After being turned in the right direction, like turtles in a race, we were free to improvise. None of us knew in advance what we'd say or how we'd say it. "But that isn't the way I'd say it!" I protested on the one occasion when Gloria sat us down to rehearse a prepared dialogue. "Well, say it the way you'd say it," she said testily.

Maybe Gloria's hope was that the scenario would grow without her intervention. Or perhaps she felt that it was dangerous to be too precise about it. In a joking way we had held her responsible when, on our first trip to the set, our van tipped into the ditch, even if her script required the bus not to tip, but to expire noisily amid clouds of smoke. (In an earlier script, however, "The driver . . . runs the bus gently off the road into a ditch.") Our real accident had the quality of a bad dream that comes true, and as we stood soberly in the rain afterwards, with green garbage bags over our heads, we had a vision of Gloria as a shamaness who had to be careful with her power. The death scene she wrote in her June 15, 1988 scenario was never used; but death was in a parallel script.

How long ago it seems (it was November 8, 1988) that Gloria's doctor told her she had a shadow on her lung; he was "worried," he said, but noncommittal when Gloria asked what that might mean. She was told on November 12th that it was lung cancer, and the doctor was pessimistic. "A year, two years maybe. *Unless* it can be cured." Gloria concentrated on the "unless" for a little over eight months.

In November she was still living with Molly in a little rented house facing Parc Lafontaine, charming and impractical. It was a struggle to find a parking place, to lug groceries home, to get across the street with sixty pounds of Molly dragging her eagerly toward the park. (Molly wrote me letters describing Gloria's problems.) Gloria's real nourishment came not from grocery bags but from the conviviality of being with friends, wherever it was, with plenty of booze to keep laughter rolling. "How come you never learned to cook?" I asked her once. "I was taking care of the dogs," she said. There were seven miniature Schnauzers in one of her previous lives and she loved them with passion, still cried at the thought of them. When she entered a state of permanent terror on November 12th, she turned against her house, connected it with her illness; maybe she'd smoked too much there, she thought, maybe the stress of moving had made her cancer-prone. She didn't want to spend a night alone there, nor did she want to ask friends to stay with her. The only place where she wanted to be, dumbly yearned to be, was my house. Her surrogate mother's house. There were many other friends who welcomed her, who raised her spirits, who behaved as good friends do in the shadow of mortal illness. Sometimes they talked to me about the helpless comfort Gloria felt in my house and in my presence, while I talked about my inability to be a mother or even the kind of friend Gloria longed for. "I'm *not* possessive," Gloria said to me one day. She had been showing symptoms of jealousy. "I'm not as bad as you think," she said mildly, while remorse ran through my veins. I'd been overexplaining my feelings as usual. The idea that I might be an element in her powerlessness against cancer had plunged me into one of my bad states; it seemed to me that I might be helping the malignant cells to spread by not giving her as much help, as much love as she needed. "I know she isn't perfect," Gloria said to a friend about *her* Mary. I wondered in what ways this Mary wasn't perfect, if they were the same imperfect ways I recognized in myself. "She's awfully cranky," said Gloria. She had asked her therapist why Mary was so cranky and the therapist said that perhaps I was going on a trip. Yes, happily my crankiness had coincided with a trip.

It was a year full of trips, and each time I was away Gloria lived like her own ghost in my house. She moved quietly from room to room, memorizing every detail, she looked at my notebooks and drawings and paintings (I'd given her the freedom of the house). She fed the cats, watered the plants, sorted my mail, made an ink sketch of the house beyond my garden, careful about the perspective. When I got back, not a fork, knife, plate, saucepan was out of place, there was a ghostly order in the entire house, the refrigerator was almost bare. She hadn't cooked, she had hardly eaten. Only one change was visible—the pieces of her life on the dining room table. She had typed them on the screen of her computer, commanded the printer to eject them on white pieces of paper. The computer held her secrets in its memory, which is much longer than an elephant's.

A few months before she died, Gloria gave me a short story she had written about a ten-year-old named Susan. Susan has been whacked by her mother with a pink plastic hairbrush because she has been "downright rude." Rudeness equals whacking; Susan gets the hairbrush, hands it over to her mother and feels no resentment. She has not yet entered her "perpetual mood of hostility." "The innocence and glorious naivete of childhood still ruled Susan's personality." She and her mother were held together by a passionate bond; snuggled in bed together on Monday nights, with earphones over their ears and chocolate bars to munch on, they listened to Lux Radio Theatre. "Susan and her mother under the gold satin eiderdown. Mother encircling daughter in her arms." A blueprint for the paradise that Gloria sought her whole life long and never found, in the arms of a mother. Even when Gloria had grown into "angry adolescence," mother and daughter still shared their old passion for the movies. "Maybe they could not talk to each other," says Susan at the end of this story, "but they could talk about what Hollywood was offering this week. A solace of sorts."

"You would have been the daughter my mother wanted," Gloria said to me one day. Or I would have been the mother that Gloria wanted. Her mother wanted an artist-daughter who was "cultivated." To her mother's wish to instill culture into her (they went to Europe, made the round of museums) Gloria was as impervious as a stone. She told me that, finally, in a supreme show of resistance, she spent whole days downstairs in the TV room watching the screen, munching junk food and smoking cigarettes. By a happy stroke of fate, her mother discovered the open sesame in the form of a newspaper ad: the National Film Board had a place open for a secretary (Gloria had been to secretarial school); she pushed Gloria out of her nest, and it was the beginning of a new life, her real life, fuelled by the old passion. She learned what she wanted and needed to learn, worked her way slowly up to scriptwriter. She had to evolve the kind of spare style scriptwriters must have, which has shed descriptive language and the language of the senses, turns all these artistic responsibilities over to the camera. The narrator must state as simply as a primer, "Seven women, all over the age of 65, are being bussed to a conference." Her senses were at the service of this simplicity; watchful and precise. Her friends say that she had the IQ of a genius. The "culture" her mother wished for her was less important to her than learning her job. "For someone so clever you are appallingly uneducated," she quotes a friend in her April 1989 letter to me. "I consider it an accomplishment, like living in Québec all my life and somehow managing never to learn French," Gloria replies. "That sort of avoidance takes a certain talent."

In her father's house there is a photograph of Gloria's paternal grandmother, a woman with a merry smile, dark eyes and a round face like Gloria's. She is wearing a wide-brimmed black hat with egret feathers standing straight up, and a coat made of some soft fur like moleskin. *She* should have been Gloria's mother, I thought, not Gloria's mother. Not I; I would have been an impatient preachy fusspot, would have provoked the same resistance, would have been resentful, too, at having my working-time interrupted by a clamouring child. Perhaps I wouldn't have laughed at all her jokes; mothers, like Queen Victoria, are not always amused. Gloria was born with the gift of laughter. She looked the part of a roly-poly clown without make-up, bright-eyed and lightning quick. She could mimic any voice, including my own; it was like having a gifted parrot at my elbow. "Oh lord, do I really sound like that?" "Oh lord, do I really sound like that?" she drawled with a wicked little smile. It made me remember how my siblings and I used to infuriate each other in just this way. Parrot mimics are delightful but human mimics are only delightful when they are mimicking someone else. "How am I going to take this?" Michelle seemed to be thinking one day on location. She was staring at a photograph of Gloria hamming it up in Michelle's costume: her white jumpsuit, her red bandanna, red sneakers, a bandage wound around her "sprained" ankle. Gloria is sitting on an upturned crate, leaning on Michelle's stick, her left hand stretched out and a big grin on her face, which has been rubbed with brown shoe polish. "Hey there," says Michelle, then smiles uncertainly. When the cat's away . . . . She had had to take the day off and a lookalike was needed to drive the bus.

When Gloria was sick she imitated what she called The Look. The Look—of deep sympathy—scared her; "it makes me fear the worst," she said. She judged her friends by their reactions to her bad news. Those who became instant non-friends looked deep into her eyes and pronounced a melancholy "Gloria," followed by a pregnant silence. Gloria could appraise the tone of comfort as accurately as a goldsmith weighing gold. At the other extreme was flippancy, happily rare. She was intransigent about professional cheerfulness, huddled into the shelter of herself stubbornly, angrily, gave short answers, refused to be cajoled. She would have none of those suave messages for coping with cancer that came in the form of how-to-do-it pamphlets, programs, get-togethers with other patients. She didn't want to fit any pattern—of terror, anger, resignation, acceptance, went silently to the oncology wing for treatments, holding tight to her own knowledge of how she felt. She would not give one milligram of herself to pretence, except in the form of the wisecracks that escaped in her doctor's office, between bouts of despair. Her wit was a safety valve but it could not help when she was alone. Even when she was sick there were times when her despair changed to gaiety; I remember a night she came to supper, took off her little cap and cradled her bald head in her arms on the kitchen table. She was worried about her visit the next day to Cape Cod with an old friend, would she get through it? We began to play a guessing game like charades; I had to guess the four-part name of her friend, syllable by syllable. By the end we were both laughing like children.

Out on the set we seemed never to stop laughing. I laughed so hard when Gloria made her hand signal for silence that there were shouts from François, "Si-lence!" (in French). Her right hand rapidly beat her thumb against her fingers; her left hand came sharply down like the gadget that marks a scene's beginning. She played practical jokes. "Gloria has set up all our chairs with their backs to each other," said Beth one day. "I wonder why." "It must have been an accident," I said. Not at all, it was one of Gloria's little traps; it caught Beth, who turned all the chairs around to face each other. Finished and unfinished laughter. I want to tell Gloria how one day when I was throwing a slipper to Emma, the Pekingese, it soared up to the ledge in the dining room that holds a row of plates, and clipped the top of one of the beautiful old platters Gloria had left me in her will. The platter turned a back somersault and dove off while I waited with a sense of doom for the crash, unbelieving when the platter hit the bare floor and didn't break. A sign that made me happy all day. It was a sign of Gloria's resiliency, of my fear, when she was alive, that she would break, falling into the abyss, that I would be partly responsible—indirectly, like the awkwardly thrown slipper hitting the platter. But Gloria had withstood a lifetime of falling into abysses and had never broken. And, once over her shock, she would have laughed her heartiest laughter.

L I N K

Question to myself: did I ever think or hope that the film was going to make chronological and dramatic sense? When I observed that Gloria was writing the scenario as we went along, this suggested a kind of growth detached from time, situated in us, changed by how we were. Did it determine the metamorphosis of the film into a fairytale? At the beginning, the filming obeyed time-laws, which in the end, as Sally was to say, "didn't matter." During the filming enough mattered to give us a sense of equilibrium: the colour and length of our hair were scrutinized, our costumes bore the before and after message: clean and dirty. And though we only saw our own scenes, some of us clung to the belief that they formed links in a story governed by time-laws. When we saw the first version of the film, in which a lot of these cherished scenes were missing, we tumbled in weightlessness. Forlorn questions floated in the air, detailed memories of those missing scenes. "Do you remember when I sang my song on the bus?" Beth asked me yesterday (May 2, 1990). "I did a little dance, and sang, and then I heard sounds in the night and got off the bus and started running toward the house. They cut that!" "You still sing and dance," I said. Well, but the end had been cut, and that was the part that explained how Beth had sought refuge with the rest of us. Another explanation that, finally, "didn't matter."

In truth, the nightly rushes situated the filmmakers, not in time, but in us—how we looked, how we were together, how convincing we were. All, of course, according to rigorous laws of colour, light and composition. Within these laws the film (like all semi-documentaries?) invented itself. No wonder Gloria put off working on the scenario. Was she waiting for the rushes to tell her how to write it? There were thirty hours, finally, of filming, and a 100-minute film inside waiting to be released, after the pieces had been endlessly rearranged, discarded and retrieved in the mysterious and somehow inevitable process of editing. That so many pieces of us are still there is a miracle. But Beth, at least, has a missing-limb syndrome activated by every missing piece of herself. "I've told my friends," she says, "that if they don't see me in the first fifteen minutes it doesn't mean that I'm not in the film!"

Unlike the audience we can't watch the film as something self-contained—this way and no other. It is true of Beth, at least, that her missing scenes were evidence to her of her existence as an actress. They made her important to herself, just as the chapter in my book has done. She had never before seen her life objectified, detached from the swarm of memories locked away, as she thought, in her head. To be looked at, to be read about. She likes the objective person. "You've made me into a real character! You've given me a real life!" she said delightedly when she read my chapter. She was prepared to see herself made visible in the film, and thinks about the shadow-film, the one that isn't there.

The shadow-film is full of us and of all the directions the film didn't take, of its logic, its realism, even of the endings we were asked to propose. Violent endings, some of them; armed men break in on us, threaten us, we are held hostage. Or they rescue us (Constance's idea). TV endings. I mused then on the fact that men immediately pop into women's heads as rescuers, and remember Gloria's indignation. "This is a film directed by women, about women, and with an all-woman cast. And they're *not* going to be rescued by men." We aren't. We are rescued by a pilot-person whose helmeted head is just barely visible at the window of the little plane.

The shadow-film also contains our ideas of how it was going to be, or how it should have been. Of how we were going to be or would like to have been? The story as we imagined it twined with the women we imagined ourselves to be. Constance, for instance, imagined herself as she would really be, lost in the wilderness, and still cannot accept the fantasy of our high spirits. "These poor old things lost in the woods," she says, "it was a survival thing, no pleasure involved. We haven't eaten well, we haven't slept well. In true life it would have been scary." I say it's supposed to be magic. "I don't see any magic," she says. There's only one scene she thinks is authentic, the one in which we've eaten "a good meal" and start to dance. "At the end, Winnie takes Cissy back to her seat and bursts into tears. I thought that was the only convincing moment in the whole film." She goes back again to the splashing scene in which Cissy, Alice and I chase each other into the lake. "You splashed and it was kind of pathetic," she says. "I was sitting on a log with my feet in the water and I thought, mon Dieu, que c'est triste!"

Constance refers to her film-self as "that dreary old woman." She isn't at all dreary, but dignified and a little sad, and it occurs to me now: wasn't this her idea of how she would be in "a survival thing"? Perhaps she thinks that her invented self, reacting to hardship, makes less sense in the context of fantasy? The "survival thing" was something that the rest of us couldn't seem to take seriously. We were all too ready to behave like children, to be, as Constance saw it, "grotesque and ridiculous." Her "made to" came from the hope that we had been directed to be childish. Not at all, I said, it was completely spontaneous. In Constance's view, old women have to be extra careful, extra dignified ("we have nothing left but our dignity," she said) in order to escape censure, and it really scared her to imagine what the audience was going to think of us. Nor did she want "fantasy" to get us off the hook.

Constance still judges according to the stern logic of her body and of her old woman's pride. She would have been hungry and aching; she wouldn't have wanted to dance or splash. Illogical and inappropriate; she uses all the reasons she can muster against our perceived lapses. But I'm glad that the essence of the splashing scene skittered away from the cutting process and made it all the way to the end. And I think that no matter how hungry or aching we were, something irrepressible in each of us would have made us splash, shout, dance because we had discovered that we were happy in each other's company. "Wasn't it beautiful? Wasn't it wonderful?" Constance still says. She is talking not only about the landscape, its calm water, fragrant woods, hills, mist and burning sun, but also about how our friendship evolved to the point where we all cried when the filming ended.

C I S S Y

Minnie Ivy Meddings is her name, but to everybody she is
Cissy. She is a compact little stooped person with eyes as blue
as a Siamese kitten's, a round head that sits close to her shoulders, short arms, and legs that stump along à la Winnie-the-
Pooh. During the filming every one of us wants to hold her hand
over rough ground or up the stone steps of the Château Borghese. We want to hug her, to protect her, above all, to be
rewarded by her impulsive smile, which is doubly merry because her teeth arch up at the centre and make an extra smile.
Her double smile seems to say, how can life contain so much
delight? Her delights are simple; she is glad to be alive after the
total eclipse of life during the war, after her stroke and the death
of her husband. Her three-part happiness lies in her only son,
John Henry, her two grandchildren, and her garden.

Out on location, Cissy sits between scenes in a folding chair;

Pierre and François squat at her feet, take both her hands. Their voices when they say, "See-see," are as caressing as the cooing of pigeons. She listens with intense seriousness to their suggestions and to Cynthia's directions for a scene, determined to do everything right. Her little hands clench. The stroke that partially paralyzed her in 1978 has left her fingers curved inward, sickle-shaped, but this doesn't prevent her now from doing, as she says in one of her scenes, "everything except knitting."

"Cissy is a true innocent," says Gloria in one of her pre-film portraits of the cast, "an honest, wise, simple, gently cheerful, enchanting human being." I think the soul that flew into Cissy's body was born before the invention of original sin (a revolting concept, in my opinion). She shed blessings on us; "God bless," she added to every farewell. "Yes, bless," were the words she remembered after an aneurism and two brain operations in the fall of 1988. Evil for her is summed up in the single word, Hitler; she still puzzles over it: how can one human being contain so much evil, "killing people like he did"? On the set she says one day, "If you want to live and thrive,/ Let the spider run alive." Out of the blue. "Live and let live," she says.

"Are you okay, Cissy?" "Ah'm okay. Are you okay?" is her invariable answer even if she is soaking wet or carsick or exhausted. I see her attention sharpen one day as her phrase, her accent float around the set; she is being imitated, and the shadow of a hurt look passes over her face. Another kind of look, inward and patient, is there at breakfast at the Château Borghese, where she sits silently next to the window. If someone speaks to her she gives a little start and gladness spreads over her face. She is eager to talk, to bring up treasures from her life, without being in the least resentful of those who talk over and past her. She has a long habit of modest but not vacant silence, while her mind works and remembers.

January, 1989. Superimposed over the summer Cissy is the Cissy lying in bed at the Neurological Centre; her head is shaved, one eye is closed and the other looks unseeingly into space, then focusses on Gloria and me. "Yes, bless," she says with a ghost of her old smile. "Yes, I do," she says a week later, when Beth and I ask if she remembers us. "I've brought you some homemade muffins," says Beth, putting them into Cissy's lap at the moment when her Cyclops eye closes, her head falls forward in sleep. Not long after that, she enters the unconscious world where she goes before another rebirth. Sometimes her legs thrash so violently that they have to be tied down, and she struggles helplessly against her bonds. Is her restlessness her only language for a great longing to stump the blocks from her apartment to her garden? Is she saying, "Let me out! Let me go home, back to my real life"? Does she know that the old people are already out there (it is the month of May) hoeing and planting and weeding? The word goes round that there's no use going to see Cissy; she is unconscious, is being fed from a tube in her stomach. Unable to imagine the power of Cissy's will, I believe that she is moving slowly toward her death, will perhaps not even notice it when it comes. Her restlessness, limbs flailing and beating against invisible constraints, when her body wanted to be free to live or to die, appears finally to be over. In the film I ask her, "Is it true you had a stroke?" "Oh yes," she answers, "I had a cerebral . . . I . . . lay flat in the hospital for . . . oh, weeks. And then one day I realized . . . I was counting the panes in the hospital. And I thought to myself this won't do. I got to get up." She got up, learned to talk and walk again, and became the Cissy we first knew.

June 4, 1990. At the Centre Hospitalier des Côtes des Neiges, 3-East, Cissy's floor, the place where hundreds of women who have lost track of time and memory can live the first of their afterlives. In the late morning, they sit asleep, belted into wheelchairs, eyes closed and mouths open. Muzak is softly playing; the nurses glide over the immaculate floor and speak in low voices. The atmosphere, calm and bright, the pleasantly coordinated colours, perhaps have the power to work their way into old bodies, even into old minds too far away to know that they are in a place where they are gently treated. Cissy, too, is asleep, with her strong arms and curled-up hands on the tray of her wheelchair. She is wearing clean white socks, a spring-green and white patterned dress with puffed sleeves; her hair is nicely done. I touch one hand and she makes a quick movement as though she were brushing away a fly. Now and then, still asleep, she changes the position of her arms, and her face has an intimation of troubled thoughts, a memory, or an effort to remember. She used to dream of trouble, she told Cynthia in her pre-film interview, "wouldn't actually dream but was restless, as if something were going to happen." John Henry has told me that she is in a time thirty years ago; when Winnie and Beth came to visit, she told them that she had cooked rabbit for lunch and gets letters from her husband. But a few days later, John Henry says that when he asked Cissy whether she remembered anyone in the film, she said, "Winnie," and this news flies joyfully from telephone to telephone. "This won't do!" Cissy must have said to herself for the second time; she must have begun to recapture memories and place them in time. In the film I say to her about her first stroke, "You're a miracle." "So they say," Cissy answers, with her thoughtful look.

June 14, 1990. I go back to the Centre Hospitalier. Alison is there, and Cynthia, supervising preparations to show Cissy the video of *The Company of Strangers*. Cissy is in her wheelchair, still in her room, wide awake, her eyes like two forget-me-nots. She looks at me fixedly, grabs both my hands and hangs on for dear life. "Take me home," she says emphatically, "take me home right away." Her look is so intense with longing that tears well out of my eyes. I try to slide my hands out of her grip but it tightens like a bird's hold on a branch. She is pushed into the TV room, still hanging on to me. There are other patients there, awake but absent, sitting behind a big table. "Who are those women at the table?" asks Cissy. A thin, deathly pale woman is making loud growling sounds and is wheeled away. Cissy is pushed close to the screen. "Cissy, do you want to see the video?" Cissy says yes. Now she has tight hold of Cynthia's hand, saws Cynthia's arm back and forth as she watches, smiling broadly, laughing, making a running commentary. "Alice," she reads on the screen. "Winnie." "I'll be damned," she says, as the photographs of her in childhood, then with her husband and John Henry, pass silently. "Cissy tensed," Cynthia tells me afterward, "when she said, 'Do you live alone, Mary?'" She tensed as she must have in the middle of our birdwatching scene, when the moment came to give the right clue for my announcement that I'm a lesbian. "Do you live alone, Mary?" she asks, and improvises the proper response to my response: "No. Well, I do at the moment, yes." In this scene, Cissy, who could have had no idea of what her exact words would be, since they had to follow my unpredictable responses, is prompted by her instinctive kindness and attentive heart, and, finally, makes us both laugh with her unexpected quip, "Yes, hid behind the closet door." We were always free to be ourselves within the framework of Cynthia's outline for a scene; Cissy was so entirely herself that it was impossible to be self-conscious in any scene with her.

Halfway through the video, Cissy begins to tear at her pink dress with her free hand, gets it off down to her waist, while she is still gazing at the screen. A clean dress is slipped over her head; she is hitched up to the IV apparatus that sustains her life now. She is restless and attentive until the end of the film. "Cissy, you were wonderful," says Cynthia. Cissy says, "We were *all* wonderful." She wants to get out of her chair; she says she can walk. The nurse and the orderly heave her up on her feet and her legs crumple under her. They are pitifully thin, without any muscles at all, unlike her strong arms and hands, almost unchanged.

We take Cissy up to the open roof, shaded by an awning, with a view of the Oratory rising from billowing trees. Women in wheelchairs with their friends and relations in attendance, flowers in cement containers. Cynthia says, "Would you like to be taken to see your garden? Would you like to have a little garden up here?" "I don't know. I don't think so. No vegetables," says Cissy.

I rewind time and stop it on the hot summer day in 1988 when I went to see Cissy in her garden. Her two plots, partly shaded by a big maple tree, were in the big community garden for seniors. Cynthia and Gloria, looking for possible members of the cast, had found her there. By now, the month of holiday dividing two blocks of filming, Cissy and I are friends, and we greet each other with cries of joy. She is one of hundreds of old people, bent over their flourishing plots, wearing rumpled clothes and hats against the burning sun. Cissy has cucumbers and onions, peppers and green beans, and pole beans with their flowers glowing scarlet against dark green leaves. An old man comes sidling along and looks at Cissy's dill. "Can I have a little of your dill?" "Yes, of course. Yes! Here, take it!" Cissy pulls up every bit of dill that I can see and hands it to him. "Is that all right? Is that enough? Are you all right?" Bowing and nodding. "Cissy! You gave him all your dill!" "Ow, it doesn't matter. It grows like a weed." "Do you know him?" I ask. "I've never seen him in my life. I don't know him from *Adam*," says Cissy and doubles up laughing. "I give them everything they want," she said about her grandchildren. "I like to spoil them." On the day of my potluck party for the cast, she brought me six jars of homemade chutney and pickles, a bag of pastry appetizers filled with meat and a bottle of Harvey's Bristol Cream.

"I'm the earthy type," Cissy said to Gloria in the pre-film interview. "I've done gardening all my life. It was an old fellow that got me interested . . . an old gardener fellow. He showed me how to prune roses, and he gave me the first thing I ever planted, whaddya call them, lilies-of-the-valley." Her sojourn in paradise, "a whole half-acre" in Dorset, planted with vegetables, with apple trees, and thousands of crocuses and daffodils, ended with the death of her husband from cancer. Her life with him in the country "was the nearest to heaven I could be," she told Gloria. When he died in 1980 she was helpless, marooned miles away from the nearest shop, unable to drive, and there were no buses. Her son, John Henry, already settled in Canada, persuaded her to come.

Her husband had helped her to walk after her first "cerebral." "He was lovely," says Cissy in the film. Now it is John Henry, the "happy-go-lucky guy" (Cissy's words) who has taken loving care of his mother since her aneurism. "It makes me sad to think that something might happen to my boy," Cissy says to Alice in the film. "I just think he was on loan to me. You know?" They are talking about their fears of being left alone, of being destitute, and Cissy begins to cry. "No, no I mustn't cry," she says while Alice comforts her. "You okay?" asks Alice. "I'm okay . . . Alice . . . yes. You . . . You okay?"

Cissy made a new life for herself in Montreal, as much of a country life as she could, living for the gardening months that finally came after the interminable winter. At first she got lost in the strange city and was careful to take along her address and a twenty-dollar bill. She made a simple grid in her head, turned right at the door of her apartment house, left, right, all the way to the mall at Côte Saint-Neige, as she called it. A good two miles there and back. "I'm good at walking," she told Gloria, "I'm not saying I walk fast. I'm a plodder." Having plodded to the mall, she carried back everything she needed for her garden. "Cissy will show you seed packets . . . like others may show you newly acquired jewels," says Gloria in her pre-film portrait. Cissy and Gloria, immediately at ease with each other in Cissy's kitchen, where chairs and table were piled with several kinds of cookies ("the Girl Guide cookies were open and asking to be invaded"), oranges, grapefruit, gumdrops, licorice, candies, peanuts, evaporated milk, and brown paper bags, still loaded. (I have a mental image of Gloria; her lips are compressed in a mischievous half-smile, she gives a quick little lick of her lips and chooses a gumdrop.) In no time they began talking about bras. Gloria's new one was digging into her back. "Oh, I hate new bras," said Cissy, "I just love wearing the old ones, all comfy, nothing hurting." Gloria's child-self, happy and confiding, met Cissy's child-self that day, and, like small children, they talked artlessly and without rivalry. They talked about their mothers. Cissy's mother had died "after lunch one day, sitting by the fire," hadn't answered when Cissy spoke to her. And Gloria's mother, sitting in a chair after lunch, had a stroke, "suddenly not answering my father, went on for two years after so much of her had died . . . . We both cry a bit for our mothers," says Gloria.

Cissy lived with her mother even after her marriage, and her husband, who was an NCO in the Army, spent his leave with her. Her mother was a "country girl," her father an engineer ("very strict") who worked at Woolridge Arsenal, a prime target for German bombs. The three Englishwomen in the cast—Cissy, Beth and Winnie—knew the terror of V-bombs and their ominous silence just before exploding. "And then it would stop and God help you," says Cissy in the film. "You just kept your fingers crossed that it was somewhere else away from you." But Cissy isn't afraid of death, she told Gloria. The Jehovah's Witnesses who climbed the stairs to her apartment had told her that she would go to heaven on Judgement Day. "Only thirty-five get to heaven," said Gloria. "Or is it 135?" Trying to steer Cissy away from Witness-influence. But Cissy can't imagine God's wrath against the billions of nonbelievers who will be cast into the flames of hell. Her God isn't vengeful; he is "someone greater than all of us, someone lots greater." "Sometimes I think when you die, that's it," says Alice in a scene with Cissy in which they are looking at the starry sky. "You're buried, and—" Cissy: "Oh, no." "—it's all over." "I think there's something further on," says Cissy, "I like to think my husband's up there. Watching me. Laughing. What a fool. What a fool I am!" A crescendo of anguish in which Cissy's hope has drained out of her. "Well, that's what they say," says Alice with her sure instinct for comfort. Cissy: "They're always watching us." Alice: "Yeah. Maybe . . . . What a beautiful moon." Cissy: "Yes, and a beautiful night, and all's well with the world, we hope . . . ."

At the wrap party that celebrated the end of filming, we were mesmerized by the vision of Cissy, dancing alone like a honeybee dancing directions, in the din and glare of flashing lights. She was wearing pink sneakers, white socks, a white cotton dress and a pink cardigan. The other dancers had left plenty of space around the circle where she shuffled her feet and spun slowly around in time to the beat. Her face, turned up, wore an expression of heavenly bliss. She held out her arms, elbows bent, fists clenched, moving to the beat, her pink sneakers shuffled and turned. She would be there till morning, it seemed, dancing her joy, while the others, a third her age, staggered exhausted off the dance floor.

MICHELLE

Michelle Sweeney was only 27 when the film was made; the rest of us ranged in age from 65 to 88. She was set apart from us by her youth, her vocation (professional jazz singer), her energy, packed into every cell of her body, emitted in a shriek like that of a speeding locomotive: "*Rock-o-o-o!*" Then for good measure, "Wah-*hoo*, wah-*hoooo!*" She must even sleep with the kind of energy it takes to recharge her aliveness. On the set, her only rival for decibels was Jacques, our sound man with the booming laugh. Michelle used her waiting-time to curl up in the back seat of any handy vehicle, for a cat-nap or with a steamy romance, *Palomino* (she read us excerpts on trips to and from the set: "Hey, listen to this!"). Or she huddled with her pal, Dawn, the second assistant camerawoman, with the face of a full-blown Peace rose. I imagined their conversation to be about men, how awful they can be but how necessary to their lives.

Before dinner at the Château Borghese, Michelle lingers in the bar, a vision of spangled satin, dark green or black, with floating stoles and flashing jewellery. This is her resplendent show-persona, whom we'll see raised to the nth power months after the end of the filming. We will be part of her audience at La Diligence, seated at a special table; we will wait after the show for the moment when she descends from the stage, makes her way straight to our table and embraces each of us in turn: her sister cast members and Cynthia, Sally, Gloria and Edna. Gloria, ashy-pale from chemotherapy, has made the immense effort to come. She is wearing a determined smile to hide the pain, and her white canvas hat tied round with a red bandanna.

Michelle's everyday energy, which she let out on location in the form of *rock-o-o-os*, *woo-hooos*, stretching, gesticulating, dance steps, alternating with an almost alarming calm, was channelled into the show-person we watched and listened to, a being in perpetual motion and sound, at times attached to a live snake that she kicked deftly out of the way, dancing with the mike as singers must do, thereby adding a whole new piece of business to the show. She was still our Michelle but was possessed by another Michelle, and the distance between us could now be measured in light years. I felt my habitual awe of performers of any kind, whether seated at a piano, juggling plates, or dancing l'Après-midi d'un Faune, transformed into their art by pure concentration.

Our Michelle wears a white mud-stained jumpsuit, and her flying black mane is held in check by a pink scarf. She tames it with a single swift whirling movement of her hands, leaving a mound of unruly hair at the back of her head. Her face is round and glowing, she is round all over, and it's a sight to see her at our première, poured into vermilion tights, swaying sinuously as she floats down the aisle, the show-person again. She is with her man and her three-year-old son, who was born crazy about music and is already an accomplished little drummer. At her Christmastime CBC show he came rushing on stage, propelled by stagefright, flung himself against Michelle's legs and hid his face against her shoulder.

Our Michelle was more ours than we were hers. I don't think she ever got over seeing the age gulf between us; certainly she never got over her wariness of me. One by one I took the names of three of her gods in vain: men, religion and family, in fatal inadvertent remarks that popped out of my mouth. When she announced in mid-summer that she was pregnant, everybody except me was in transports of excitement. It was just like *The Golden Girls*, in which I usually ally myself with Sophia, Dorothy's tough little mother, who is as unsentimental as a Sicilian goat. All except Sophia go over the top at the news that Dorothy's daughter is pregnant.

Michelle, though she knows how to raise hell, is, according to Gloria's first summary, "God-fearing, spiritual. She knows what's right and what's wrong and she tries to do right but doesn't always succeed. She reads the Bible (and seems to think this is *the* guide to Life), was raised in a church." That is, by a God-fearing grandmother, an imposing person with a regal bearing, according to the photograph Michelle showed us. Michelle's mother broke down under the burden of racism, "had a series of nervous breakdowns," Michelle told Gloria, but has lived happily with the same man for the last twelve years. Racism, the continuing threat; in West Virginia Michelle's family was told to sit in the back of the club where she was singing (she refused). She herself was turned away at a Montreal bar. Out on location I could feel her wariness; could she trust us?

In the film one sees a gentle, confiding Michelle, except in the first scene, the breakdown of our bus. In this scene, Michelle, who in Gloria's first scenario is "in a furious rage," merely shouts, "Drat! Doggit!" when she sprains her ankle, and mutters, "I can't believe I'm walking around in the woods with all these old . . ." Impatience is her flaw, she has told Gloria in the first interview. The gulf between herself and "these old . . ." is visible in the luminous clarity of her face, the difference between her face and ours, which will never again have the texture, smooth and firm as silk, of youth. In each scene Michelle plays with one of us, this visible difference is there as a presence—the Years, the Ages of Woman. In the scene in which Michelle and I are talking about the sleeping Constance, a fourth presence appears distinctly: the shadow of death, a dramatic persona with arms outstretched to span the years between Michelle and me and between me and Constance.

In each scene with one of us, Michelle listens intently, draws us out; in two scenes, her wish is like that of a blood donor, to make a transfusion of her own freedom and high spirits, to retrieve our own, which lie in the past. She persuades Beth to loosen her collar and take off her wig; to Catherine she says, "Let yourself go—Yay! Yay!" Even with a sprained ankle that slows down her body, her spirited youth bears us up, makes us behave like people half our age, sets off the scene: "Is anybody there?" in which Beth, Alice, Cissy, Mary cry "We're all alive!" Throughout the film Michelle sounds the motif of life, and Constance the motif of death, echoed by her interest in the dead birds in my drawings, and, like a death, her inability to hear the song of the white-throated sparrow. Michelle, our comico-serious jester, brings out our ability to be happy in the present, culminating in the card game near the end of the film, in which Constance, who thinks she has won, laughs a merry peal of laughter. "I've got nothing," she says. "She laughs. She laughs. I don't believe it," cries Michelle. The entire film is summarized in Constance's laughter and Michelle's joyful disbelief. She has not believed that Constance wants to be happy; "I think all the desire's left," she says to me. But there is a movement toward happiness in the film; it sweeps Constance along: "I'm very happy here. Aren't you?" she says to Winnie. They are wading along the edge of the beach, Constance's white dress floats lightly on the water. She has remembered her child-self, here in this very spot. The happiness retrieved by memory gives life to present happiness and the strata of time are compressed into a single moment. Every one of us except Michelle has a scene of remembering; about her own life she says nothing. "Do you sing?" Catherine asks her. "Sometimes ... [singing] I love ... is a real love. Wooh!" She laughs, and changes the subject to Catherine's life. She speaks only two words that resonate with her past, when Alice is putting "a shiny leaf" on her ankle to ease the swelling. "Who gave you this remedy?" asks Michelle. "My grandmother," says Alice. "Your grandmother." Michelle's words are spoken so gravely that we know without knowing that her grandmother has the power to heal, and that Michelle, like Alice, was brought up in her ways.

MINIATURE: SALLY

Sally wore several hats, all at the same time. Her title of Assistant Producer was a double portmanteau word; she was one of the deciding fates, had the extra responsibility of knowing where we were at all times, or rounding us up, singly, in pairs or in groups, ridding us of extraneous pieces of non-costume and remembering where they were hidden, teaming up with Alison in this delicate task, patient at the querulous sound of "where is my . . . ?" Sally was keeper of a big notebook, which I once had the honour of holding on my knees for a few seconds in her red Buick. Though I didn't dare look into it, I knew that it was full of vital information about the order and substance of scenes, as essential to a film as the black box of an airliner. Sally communed with her black book and watched a scene in progress with eagle eyes. For us she had a look that arrived as rapidly as a hummingbird, perched on a face, with a concentrated smile that screwed up her eyes and compressed her mouth. It required a small forward movement of her head and of her triangular nose, like the ones in profile on Greek vases. Her smile was a reward, less precise than Cynthia's "good," but of equal value. During long hours of waiting, Sally was one of my objects of study: her reddish hair, short-cropped at the back and sides, sat on her head like a Persian kitten with one paw draped over her left eye. She had a habit of wearing a sweatshirt over a longer, different-coloured tee shirt, which made her look like a French or Italian flag, held vertically.

Sally's power as éminence grise was exercised in places that were off limits to us. Out on location she held secret talks with those of us who had problems, questions about the appropriateness of scenes (our dignity at stake?) or the "why am I waiting around all day without doing anything?" syndrome. One day she called a conference at the apartment at which the seven of us over 65 were asked our views about sex. Gloria was there, hoping I'd proclaim lesbian rights and disappointed by my silence, which she blamed on everybody except me. They hadn't drawn me out, she complained; they had treated me as though I were invisible. I felt her hopeful eyes on me, quavered out that I wasn't interested in sex any more and looked fixedly at the floor. Most of the others agreed shyly that sex is nice . . . perhaps if Mr. Right came along (a scene to this effect was later shot with Winnie, Alice and Beth) . . . for they didn't want to give the idea that they were too old or had completely stopped thinking about men. (I let pass this ideal moment for saying that I hadn't completely stopped thinking about women.) At times, they were lonely, some of them. Constance, however, said energetically that she was glad not to have to think about all that messy business any more, closed her eyes and went to sleep.

Sally was to me the most mysterious of the three fates, since I felt shy with her and only ventured to talk to her about her life as a horsewoman, which I might have guessed simply from the way she moved and squinted her eyes. She told me about a

124

woman who conveyed the message of control to a frisky horse merely by the way she sat on its back and held the reins. Sally, too, seemed to be holding the reins loosely, with sensitive hands, looking keenly from under the brim of a black velvet cap. If she was tense inside at the thought of imminent water-jumps, hedges and five-foot gates, her tenseness was translated by the horse into reassurance and faith in its power to clear every obstacle.

SMALL SPACES

"Sing us a song, Michelle," I say on our last trip from the set in the grey van. Michelle thinks; we wait silently, and she sings:

> Everything must change
> Everything stays the same
> Everyone must change
> Nothing stays the same
> The young become the old, oh yes!
> and mysteries do unfold
> but never much too soon
> Nothing and no one goes unchanged
> There are not many things in life you
> can be sure of except rain comes from the clouds
> and the sun lights up the sky
> and the hummingbirds do fly

Winter turns to spring
and the wounded heart will heal
'cause that's the way of time.
Nothing stays the same
There are not many things in life
you can be sure of
except rain comes from the clouds
the sun lights up the sky
and hummingbirds do fly.

The vans, the blue Ford (Catherine's), the red Buick (Sally's) were spaceships from time to timelessness, journeys within timelessness, to places with water in their names: Boileau, Huberdeau, la Rivière Rouge. To places abandoned or on the edge of fatal change. The grey van, our flagship, has replaced the capricious red van that disgraced itself on the first day of shooting. It was pulled out of the ditch with difficulty by a tow truck and went into exile and oblivion. Just as well, because the grey van is more suitable to its cargo of white and grey heads and we can, in an emergency, fetch up comfortably against any part of its padded interior.

Picture us after a 5:30 wake-up call, hungry and morose. We straggle out the front door of the Château Borghese, wobble down the stone steps, hanging on to each other. Alison Burns, a production assistant, is standing in the mist by the grey van, like a groom holding a mighty draft horse; the mounting block, a Granny Smith-coloured "half-apple," is on the ground; we are tugged and pushed up the step. "Where's Michelle?" In due time Michelle comes sombrely down, mumbles a greeting, falls into the back of the van, curls up with her face toward the corner and sleeps. In Montreal she sings at night and she is not going to pretend to be alert and cheerful at 5:30 a.m. Alison appears to be the only cheerful one, though she may have made a trip to Montreal and back the evening before and has certainly been up since well before dawn. She is the film factota, laden with a heavy grab-bag of responsibilities. She drives, sitting very straight, with imperturbable skill. In the van, her walkie-talkie, which is usually slung low on one hip with the antenna shooting up at a jaunty angle, lies quietly at her side, ready to crackle hoarse commands. And Alison, at the sound of its voice, hustles us into (or out of) the van, back to (or away from) the set. The black box is her master; it can command her to look for something left behind or to bound across a field like an Irish setter with ears flying, to retrieve, to fetch, to carry. Like an Irish setter, she has long wavy red hair; she gallops through the dew-soaked grass, wearing her shiny Wellingtons and shorts, with her red hair, her limbs like an adolescent boy's, in perpetual motion. Flying arms and legs, flying handwriting. One day at the Château Borghese I find a message from Alison poked under my door. It fills a whole page. "<u>Mary</u> you can wear your dirty clothes Thanks Alison." The letters balloon like spinnakers racing before the wind. The A in Alison is like a sailing frisbee. Only the line under Mary, and the anchor of the T in "Thanks," keeps the message from flying off the page.

At times, Alison confesses, she gets into real tizzies out there. Perhaps she's had to make one of her unscheduled trips to Montreal to pick up something or someone, perhaps she has been asked once too often, where is my hat, coat, pocketbook? At these times she turns pale, as redheads do, her blue eyes hint at suppressed desperation, but she doesn't start screaming or reply angrily. Her voice becomes a little louder, her eyes wider, her movements as hectic as a jumping jack's. Somehow or other she has learned self-control, maybe as one of a family of seven children, in the rough-and-tumble in which they sometimes snapped and snarled at each other like a litter of puppies. In the van, her family saga enlivens our trips: the Burns boys and girls jumbled together, fighting and playing like the children in my favourite children's books, and growing up with a sense of bodily ease.

Trips from Montreal to St. Jovite in the grey van. The green-eyed Laura Oliva, another of the production assistants, is driving. She is as beautiful as Venus rising from the sea, has a meridional sense of time, like Angelo, the other Italian. The van meanders, takes siestas or puts on dizzying bursts of speed. Constance is sitting in the front seat. I see her delicate blue-veined hand reach out and gently stroke the bear's head of Oscar, Laura's chow, who is sitting up and whining uneasily. Back and forth, back and forth, Constance's hand moves. "Couche, Oscar!" says Laura sharply and he sinks down. He is imprinted on Laura and neither looks at nor listens to anyone else.

On trips to the set, Cissy, fighting carsickness, sits in the front seat of the van. Her voice pipes up when we play the alphabet game. "Your turn, Cissy!" Cissy jumps. "Ow! I went on a trip and took . . . an alligator, a—a—a boa constrictor, a—a—a ["catamaran," whispers Alison] catamaran, and a—a—a *donkey*," she says delightedly. In the tight little space of the van, voices come out of the backs of heads, dramas blow out of these disembodied voices. Sometimes my subversive opinions issue from the back seat where I usually sit between Beth and Michelle, and run into Alison's religious beliefs or Michelle's family loyalties. It's so easy to hurt people's feelings! I discover in our closed space that I have to watch my tongue, stay away from the sacred or provocative subjects (feminism). Much pleasanter is the cocoon of prudent silence, I discover. Let Gloria, who is so fearless and eloquent, fight for the Cause.

Sometimes, though, the van seems to contain a charge of dynamite and the fuse to set it off. The other spaces, too: Catherine's blue Ford, Sally's red Buick, the dinner table at the Château Borghese. I am a mere spectator, along with Winnie, at a splendid battle in the blue Ford in which Catherine, the Roman Catholic nun, is pitted against Constance, the disenchanted Catholic. It is about Church education in Québec, "a subject I really know something about," says Constance. Winnie is rooting for Catherine, I for Constance. We are in the back seat, straining our ears for every word. I am delighted to learn that nuns can lose their cool. "You're so prejudiced I can't talk to you!" cries Catherine. ("She's so prejudiced!" Constance says to me later.) Winnie suggests from the back seat that it may rain tomorrow. Constance turns her head slightly. "Heh heh, you're trying to change the subject, aren't you?" Constance loves arguments, gathers herself together like a racehorse at the gate, leans forward tensely. She's off! This happens at the Château Borghese, too; shock waves run down our ranks at the dinner table. Constance is looking across at me sternly and saying, "Women died so that you could vote!"

In my mind's eye I touch the interiors of our spaces: the matter-of-fact blue upholstery of the Ford, the plushy redness of the Buick. Sally driving, Catherine beside her; Edna, Gloria and I squeezed into the back seat. The talk flies back and forth; Catherine is well into an impassioned account of how she made her vow of celibacy. Gloria puts in a word for a seventh-century edict, before which nuns and priests weren't required to be celibate. Pitted against Gloria's sharp weapons, Catherine, like an octopus, emits a dense cloud that floats back over the barricade of the headrests, and puts Gloria out of commission. At which we are reduced to helpless snorts. "Catherine," I manage to say, "I can't understand a word you're saying." "Well, you should have heard me ten years ago," says Catherine. She tells me much later that this is her strategy "when someone's trying to pin me down."

The smallest spaces—the turquoise blue portable Jiggs toilets, and their more impressive kin, the washrooms at the Rivière Rouge, the Town Hall at Huberdeau, and across the road, the washroom in the apartment that is our refuge during long waiting periods. One of the many pieces of thoughtfulness on the part of Sally and Alison is to anticipate: before we leave the Château Borghese (an elegant restroom there aglow with marble and brass), the apartment, before scenes, before we climb into the van at the end of the day. Sometimes, for those of us who have turned up our noses at the idea of a last trip to the Jiggs, the van makes a detour to the apartment before heading home. The Jiggs wakes all my dormant hang-ups about being seen on my way to a toilet. The Jiggs at Location 1 is highly visible, in a hollow not far from the old house. I go through elaborate rituals, gazing around as though I may see an interesting bird, pausing at the food tent as if my intention is to make myself a peanut butter sandwich. At the lake location, you can stroll carelessly along a woodsy road and your goal will be discovered only if there is someone ahead of you. At Location 3, trapped behind our bus parked in the middle of the road, waiting for its death scene, with the Jiggs so far out of sight that Sally runs a shuttle (the red Buick) to take us there, I amble up the road, ostensibly for a nature walk, to pee in the woods. Which is how I happen to see the raccoon's skull, half- hidden in moss, and the owl's face drawn on the back of the little toad.

"Get out, mate," says Beth to Edna in the grey van, giving her a little slap on her black-clad behind. By then we have all learned the compressed intimacy of the van or car-spaces, acquired during the times when we have been squashed together like hotdogs. In the red Buick, for instance, my backseat position between Edna and Gloria, sitting with my legs strad- dled over the big middle hump and rocked with every curve against one or the other. It is impossible to see out the wind- shield because of the towering headrests, or to see out the side windows because of a body on either side of me, and with every involuntary movement I make to left or to right I am hyper- conscious of the body that touches mine. In Edna's I find comfort, for as a nurse, mother, grandmother, she has held bodies of all shapes and sizes with kindly ease. In Gloria's, I feel a total awareness that a right-hand curve will bring me closer to her without her moving a centimetre, feel her spreading wave of contentment, almost as though she is actually saying, "m-m-m," which vanishes when I am thrown against Edna by a left-hand curve. In the front seat, Sally and Constance are pursuing a serious conversation, unaware of the little drama being played out directly behind them. But it comes to pass out there that in whatever space, large or small, bodies melt and touch, spontaneously hug, hold hands, lock arms, with no sense of fear or caution or impending aftermath. The vans and cars merely hasten this process.

Small spaces—those where choices are made: to sit down at which round table with an empty chair, at the Town Hall in Huberdeau where we have lunch. Sometimes, when I wander in after making a trip to the restroom, there is a difficult choice to be made, as in tic-tac-toe, in the form of at least three empty spaces, one of them at the table where Cynthia, Sally and Gloria sit, and from which Gloria is shooting me an inviting look. Which I ignore, walking resolutely toward the tables where my buddies sit, wavering, and plunking myself into the chair next to Constance, who, as often as not, says, "Are you going to sit next to this old deaf woman?" Constance always appraises the desserts—apple turnover, custard pudding—with her connoisseur's eye and smiles her special smile of gourmet pleasure when she brings one back to the table. "You're not having any dessert? Why not?"

"Give us a program to keep seven old women in stressful conditions alive and happy," I imagine the planners saying to a computer. How many hours can they work? What's the earliest bearable wakeup time? Latest wrap-time? How many restrooms? Jiggs? What do they like to eat? Most important, where are they going to spend the time that they're not on the set? The word "apartment" appears commandingly on the screen. "Near the Town Hall at Huberdeau." I suspect that the Film Board built an old red barn just for us; at any rate, an untenanted apartment is inside it, a simply furnished haven with a kitchenette and fridge, where we can play cards, drink coffee, where one of us (usually me) can collapse on the big bed that almost fills the adjoining bedroom. I lie there and listen to the laughter and cries of triumph or accusation on the other side of the partition, or, supine on my back on the narrow strip of floor, I do Edna's stretching exercises, while the others play King-in-the-corner and 31. Constance, meanwhile, indifferent to baby games (she admits to being a very good bridge player), settles into the reclining chair, tilts her head back and is almost immediately asleep. She might have posed for one of the fifteenth-century paintings in which saints and soldiers sleep and dream: St. Joseph, St. Ursula, the centurions in *The Sleeping Watch* (the one in armor looks like Constance) motionless in sleep-space. Constance's closed eyes, like theirs, seem to have arrested time and her heartbeat.

A final space, the blue tent with a groundcloth, set up for anyone on the set who craves calm, where it is possible to spend an hour or so on a chaise longue in a state of suspended animation, and any conversation with another reclining body is taboo. I stretch out there; a scene is being shot somewhere beyond my hearing, and all those waiting in the shade of the house are in a silent trance. At times a big cloud passes over the sun and I pull my coat over me, and then the sun bursts free and spreads its heat. Idly, my mind registers sounds: the flapping of the roof, like a big bird taking off, the sighing of trees in the wind, bird songs:

kwaw kwaw
chigger, chigger, chigger
pee-chuk, chuk-tsip
gee-up, gee-up, zuh, chik chikka chikka gup
kwaw kwaw

CATHERINE

Catherine's mentor for her Doctoral studies compared her to an octopus, she told me at our taping session in which she recounted her life. I was startled, since I had used the same image when I was writing this book: a scene in which Catherine was in the front seat of Sally's red Buick, and Gloria was in back. Gloria had posed Catherine a question about her vow of celibacy, and Catherine answered it with one of her impenetrable octopus-clouds. Now I said, "Octopuses are very intelligent; they emit inky clouds to confuse the enemy." "I do that when someone is trying to pin me down," she answered with a little smile. Recently she sent me a paper, "Motivational Terrain of Catherine M. Roche," which she concludes by saying, "I certainly should be able to perform better being a more integrated 'octopus,'" with a note below from her professor: "Wonderful image. Resonate with it!"

So the octopus has become Catherine's totem-animal and my fear—that she might not admire octopuses as much as I do—was groundless. Even as a child she was one, either waving her many arms around to explore the world, or shooting away, folded up like an umbrella, in the shelter of her cloud. For a while, she says, people thought she was stupid; in fact, she was in hiding, waiting for the times when she "got a lot of grace." She was reading a children's magazine and suddenly found a "world there"; she listened to a record of music she had heard at her dancing class, and understood that music and movement are synonymous. She saw a field of yellow flowers, and yellow became the colour that means most to her. She translates other colours into yellow: our bright blue tents out on the set, "they were yellow, weren't they?"

If you pressed Catherine for an explanation, "How can your mind change bright blue to yellow?" she would back up her answer with the latest scientific theories and produce evidence from the church fathers; she would send out an octopus-cloud. It is one of her many talents to address any subject so voluminously that a respectful silence is the only possible response. She is able to talk for an hour without pausing for breath. If I cry, "Catherine!" she can drink a cup of tea, pick up her story in the middle of the sentence where she left off and continue for another hour. At times during her seance with my tape recorder I drifted into sleep, knowing that her words were being preserved. For instance, the following: "I was taken to a field of yellow flowers and had the feeling of being freed and of being alive and of being in my element. And now I can be driving along and see a field of yellow flowers and I'm free all of a sudden again and I get the same transcendent lift." Yellow, I think, is to Catherine the colour of grace, and the process of "getting grace" or of having it already, is a fundamental part of her narrative. "And Daddy somehow got a special grace because he was a delightful personality, he had inner grace just shining out of him." "My mother, Marie, became very grace-filled and she loved yellow."

A film based on Catherine's taped narrative might begin with an overview of a forest, nothing but "trees and trees and trees and trees," and somewhere among the trees, a patch of mud, scattered with houses. This is, or will be, the mining town of Flin Flon, with a population of 200 souls. There are no streets and no mine. Catherine's father brings his family there. The town leaders hire draft horses to haul the houses into tidy rows and put down sidewalks. Her father supervises the building of the mine. He and the parish priest, "who had a tremendous devotion to the Sacred Heart, built a church and then a better one." Somehow or other, Flin Flon becomes a miniature cultural centre; "the teachers and the young Americans who created this community, they'd put on musicals and plays and have wonderful creative social parties." At the heart of this life is Enid, Catherine's stepmother. (Catherine's mother had died in a little mining town when Catherine was three.) For two years Enid teaches Catherine and her brothers at home, using her homemade Montessori method, and the rigours of school later must have come as a rude shock. Catherine describes Enid: "she loved laughter and was a lot of fun, she was very beautiful and very ladylike." Here she is, in Catherine's memory, standing at the foot of a great tree, "pulling down pine cones." She begins to laugh; she cries out, "These strong women of the north!" In Flin Flon, Enid has three daughters and a son in quick succession, and "live-in" girls to help her. Catherine disappears into one of her octopus-clouds. To the observer, this might appear to be sulking, but, Catherine explains, "I didn't sulk, just became very 'virtuous and holier-than-thou or self-sacrificing.' I was coldly rude but didn't lose my temper. I was too pious!" "If I wanted to help for something like a dinner party," she goes on, "I was told to help by keeping out of the way. But I was supposed to do the boring chores." She makes a careful distinction between this more mature state of being (she was six) and her real sulkiness at three when, after her mother's death, she lived with her grandmother in Salt Lake City. It was at this time that Enid, now married to Catherine's father, also lived in the house. Her presence changed Catherine's loneliness to joy; when she came home from teaching school, Catherine and her brothers rushed into her outstretched arms crying, "Enid! Enid! Enid!"

Now in Flin Flon, Catherine is one of seven children. She takes tender care of her little sisters, but wears her look of "pious self-sacrifice" as she does the dishes with *Anne of Green Gables* propped on the windowsill. Enid, busy with the little kids and the housekeeping, still has time for teaching, but is "cool now and psychologically correct." "If I was more vocal," says Catherine, "I would have said to Enid, 'yes, but I want you to love me, hug me, even fight with me' . . . but I didn't say that." Eventually, she makes an equation to ensure the love of God, a circular movement of love given and received: "The whole essence of religious life is to believe that God loves you. You always feel good when you know that someone loves you—this is a luxury, so you have to believe."

In Flin Flon people walked everywhere and stopped every few seconds to exchange greetings. For Catherine, who was "very shy, very," this was an ordeal; she practised talking on the streets of Flin Flon, and filling a silence, making her voice heard, was a proof of courage. More than that, she was learning the meaning of community. Catherine, aged six, was already used to mining towns; she must have been born with an instant sense of bustle and hurry. "My brother was born in one mining town and when they were living in another mining town my mother went into Salt Lake City and had me and we were back in the mining town again." She also seems to have been born with her gift for seeing time not as a continuum, but as a receptacle like a water-filled sphere, in which snowflakes swirl and settle, always in a new order. "My father," she says, "moved up to Salt Lake and went to college there and became a mining engineer and a construction engineer while working as a bouncer in a theatre and married my mother and was a football player." After a dizzying sentence like this I am surprised to find images as clear as photographs; to find, too, that there is a beginning, in which Catherine was born, and that she had a real mother until she was three. She has a memory of her mother giving her an apple: "it was all brown and she just cut out the brown and I can remember to this day the light and the joy that came into my life with this beautiful calm smiling presence." Soon after that Catherine was taken to a hospital where her mother lay on an army cot, dying of peritonitis. "They told me to kiss her and I did and there was absolutely no response ... she had a dead baby in her womb but I didn't know she was dying and nobody talked about it." But her mother had been able to say to Enid, "I want you to take care of the children."

Strong guideposts stand out in the forest of Catherine's memories: father, mother, stepmother, people she adored. And once "religion took hold of her," a rosary of priests, nuns, Jesuit teachers, mother superiors, materialized to help her out of her Sloughs of Despond. Catherine was born, I think, with the family motto, "Dieu est ma roche," clearly visible over her infant head. Her stepmother converted to Catholicism; her father was responsible for building the Catholic church in Flin Flon. The town was a crossroads for Oblate missionaries, "canonizable marvellous missionaries," Catherine calls them. No wonder religion took hold of her: "it was comforting, it was strengthening, I guess I got a lot of grace." One of the missionaries, the Bishop in The Pas, was so handsome that she thought of him as the incarnation of Jesus. Catherine "adores men and doesn't want to push them around," says Gloria in her 1988 notes about the cast.

"Do you thrive on ordeals?" I ask Catherine in one of our

film scenes together. Catherine prefers the word "task" to "ordeal." "You sometimes do them," she says, "because you want to live the life you want to live. And . . . you don't let yourself get stopped by things." Catherine's preparation for any task is to build herself up, just as in Montreal she built up her body in workouts at Nautilus. Every task exercises her in some way and leads to something harder. In Flin Flon she made herself talk; later, in college, she was on the debating team. She built up her voice until she was able to give singing lessons and sing in choral concerts. She has always been good at sports; indeed, I think of her life as a kind of decathlon in which she has had to get the ten disciplines in harmony with each other. Did they think she was stupid as a child? Well, she'd show them. At school she was called "the homework angel." Homework, training, rules and theories to keep herself and her ideas from flying to pieces. Her lifelong struggle has been to make order out of her complications, which have regularly plunged her into depressions and emotional problems. "You were pulled so many ways and nobody seemed to know how to help you to integrate this into one really meaningful life," she says of the time before becoming a nun. Catherine is still at her work of integrating. Often, when some part of her seems to wobble or crumble, she erects a scaffolding of theory—musical, pedagogical, philosophical. Theory braces her.

Listening to Catherine, I think theory is all very well but Catherine as teacher is the child who learned from Enid how enthusiasm and attention are generated in children. How, when attention (love) is withdrawn, it is a kind of death. "There was absolutely no response"; this is how she describes the moment when she kisses her dying mother's cold face. No response—a court of no appeal. For Catherine, it was to be cast into darkness, it marked times when there were no answers to her questions, it precipitated her failures. Almost at the end of her narrative she says, "Now I haven't recounted on the tape all the failures I've had but it's dotted with one shattering failure after another, after which you get up and make something out of it, I don't know how except if you have decided to go into this vocation what's the use of stopping? I don't want to go dead inside." Real failures or her sense of failure? For years she was caught in the machinery of the Montreal school system, had head-on collisions now and then with principals and commissioners, saw colleagues die of heart attacks and have nervous breakdowns. "In one school," she says, "if you went out of your room you locked the door; you put the straight-faced look on your face in the hall and you didn't look to right or left. Two teachers had had their heads kicked in, there were drugs, people would walk in off the street, twice my wallet was stolen." In a difficult classroom, Catherine's technique to calm down her kids and get their attention was "to spend one out of three periods just sitting with them, not talking, not answering them when they shouted and yelled. I'd hold back on them then they'd produce art like you wouldn't believe." While art and music were being squeezed out of the curriculum she clung to her knowledge that they are instrumental in learning. (Enid had taught her this.) Catherine emphasizes that in many ways the school system was good, but in this area nobody listened to her: "they picked people who weren't going to rock the boat."

In Catherine's despairing periods, when she cries out for help and there is no response, somebody always comes along, as they do in fairytales, a guide. Her father, Enid, the missionary she identified with Jesus ("I gazed at him he was so magnificent") were guides. They help her to get grace or to encourage the birth of a new soul. "A new superior in Montreal a very very deep woman of great wisdom a shy woman a mystic-type helped me to find my soul. She was the spiritual mother of my new soul." Catherine adds souls just as a tree adds rings. The spaces between rings mark journeys between souls; her times of failure hastened the appearance of a guide and the growth of a new soul. When she feels lost in a wilderness of choices and indecision, she makes the decision of her life. She trudges up Atwater

Avenue in the rain, saying a prayer, "Lord, if you want me you better give me a *good welcome*," rings the doorbell of the Society of the Sacred Heart. The Reverend Mother must have dreamt that a tall young woman with a strong face would come to the door, looking for her vocation; she tells the portress to let Catherine in. "You'd better go she's come from quite a while," she says. "From quite a while." The heroine has been on an arduous journey; she is recognized and welcomed, she sails through all the interviews that test her determination. "'Well,' says the American provincial, 'You'll need your passport.' I said, 'Well, I don't need it I'm American.' 'Oh,' she said, 'so am I,' and that was our interview." "So then I went with a *great* weight off my chest," Catherine continues. "I felt really happy and cornered by God . . . I felt the world was just kind of a *dead* place, and if I went here I'd know that everything was God's will, the only thing I could find that would solve my problem knowing that I was doing what God wanted."

About an hour into her narrative, Catherine says, "I'm going as fast as I can!"—misinterpreting my signals, which were supposed to suggest a break for tea. I think of Alice and the Red Queen, who are running hand in hand. "And the Queen went so fast that it was all she could do to keep up with her, and still the Queen kept crying, 'Faster! Faster!'" Looking over my transcript of the tape I stop and breathe deeply, as Catherine does in her meditation sessions, when I come to milestones: Vatican II, Catherine's realization that "music was what I hungered for," her teaching experiences in inner-city schools. The Catherine we know is the nun who was set free by Vatican II, dressed, except on location, in primary colours, and sometimes toting a bottle of Chivas Regal. She speaks her mind; she has a tone of authority and the evident habit of being listened to that I associate with most of the teachers I know. She is still entirely her own woman, not loony like the rest of us with the contagion of happiness. Her real schedule isn't here but far away with her choral group, and will take her to Europe. "We evolved slowly after Vatican II," she says on her tape, "from totally cloistered to a point where we are all now a sort of institution in ourselves. A lot of nuns living alone a lot carrying on a very creative original apostolate." "They know how to leave us free," she says, "and my friends who have suffered from an authoritarian upbringing look at me and wonder . . . oh, this nun look at her she's travelling all over look how free she is." Vatican II freed her for a life in music; "totally cloistered," the nuns' regime consisted of prayer and teaching, with little time for music. "On feast days," she says, "we would have a musical 'treat,' music was an extra: one of the 'arts d'agrément'." "All these years," she says, "music was what I hungered for. It was the most complete thing to teach it was the most personally involving total thing it takes your emotions it takes your brain you think in sound when you're doing music it takes your background you have to understand people culture . . . ."

Catherine, at one with her Walkman, thinking in sound, excited now at the prospect of "going back in the educational world in Stockton" where she wants to show kids "with ghetto mentalities" that great music can heal differences between people, just as it has untangled some of the knots in her. Musical leit-motifs have always sounded in the forest, like Papageno's magic flute, beckoning her toward the appointed time when she was ready for her complicated new soul. Now she is preparing herself again, in training for "the most complete thing to teach," a fresh career in music that will make use of all her faculties and beliefs. "I just have to know . . . keep on learning," she says. "I don't know when it started, that search that I went through for finding some kind of life that had meaning. Somewhere along the line I learned the word integrity."

"Look how free she is, and look at me tied down," people say enviously about Catherine, "people who wonder what makes you tick how can you live this life? People whom I've just met will look at you and think well how do you manage your sex life?" (Gloria's question about celibacy—a leading question that led nowhere?) Catherine takes time out to laugh and then assumes her octopus-persona: "To me if your religion isn't a total thing if you aren't living a rich intellectual life at the level that you can and an emotional life and your sex life if you are not reaching out to people with, you know, generous interest and want to let them get involved in your life what have you got to give your God? But the biggest help I've found has been using the oriental meditation of the mantra . . . ."

Any hint of Catherine's unspoken life is lost in a cloud of people and events: the guides who help her on her way, like the "apostle" of meditation in Montreal, and those in the past. People who have helped her by hindering her. Burn-outs in teaching, like the periodic fires that leave forests ready for new growth, learning programs—all part of her quest "to know." Again I think of Alice and the Red Queen who are running so fast that their feet are flying out behind them. When they stop, Alice finds herself "sitting on the ground, breathless and giddy. The Queen propped her up against a tree, and said kindly, 'You may rest a little now.' Alice looked round her in great surprise. 'Why, I do believe we've been under this tree the whole time! Everything's just as it was!'" Catherine has been running since she was born, running against time, against herself (she is both Alice and the Red Queen), against the deadness inside or out-side. She will run until she dies. She has so much to do still! She wants to emulate her "old aunt of 101 years. They say I'm very like her." They met and talked in June 1990, and straightened out the family roots. Another meeting that linked generations, like Constance's meeting with the old nun who remembered Constance as a child singing in the convent choir.

In *The Company of Strangers* photographs of the cast as children and young women pass silently. The intense life of these past selves overwhelms me; they, too, are semi-documen-taries, the partial evidence that remains of the past hidden away in our present bodies. They tell us what we sometimes doubt, and what other people doubt—that we were once young. The images of Catherine pass: she is a sturdy, serious child, she is an irrepressible tomboy; she is the newly fledged nun in her habit, smiling a newly minted smile. Transported. But she is always the same Catherine; "everything's just as it was." For I see that smile in the film when she stands on the pontoon of the little seaplane come to rescue us (months before, she had told Gloria that one of her dreams was "to be at a lake, to be able to fly"), and cries, "I did it!" Did she feel the same kind of *transport* when she flew over our landscape and landed on the calm lake? Her greatest smiles express her exuberance when she has accomplished a difficult task, whether she is dressed in a nun's habit or in her rumpled film costume, when she can cry triumphantly, "I did it!"

C Y N T H I A

"Yes, m'dear," says Cynthia. Her mind has turned swiftly from Argus-eyed watchfulness, with a movement of her whole body, a bracing of her feet, as though her only purpose in life now is to listen to my question. "Is it OK if I say . . . ?" This has to do with a forthcoming scene, over which I've been mulling. "Of course," says Cynthia indulgently, "say anything you want to say." Or she squats down and takes hold of both Cissy's hands. "Cissy, my darling," she says. Cissy comes out of her waiting state, in which her gaze is directed at a faraway place between land and sky. Now her entire attention is signalled by an eager smile: "Yes! Yes!" Leaning forward, and looking suddenly as though she is about to run a race. "Now, Cissy, I want you to . . . ." She wants Cissy to arrive in any way she pleases at a given destination. Her indulgence extends to times when Cissy and the rest of us never make it to the destination, when the temptation to wander away has been too great, or when one of us has stumbled over a scruple. (Constance, before a scene in which I'm supposed to tell her that I'm a lesbian: "I don't see why we have to talk about all these things.")

Cynthia allows us to wander, even to get nowhere. A scene that doesn't reach its destination may contain a few drops of the essence of our selves, and both Cynthia and Gloria believe that this essence can be refined into poetry. Destinations, objectives are stated in Gloria's scenario but we can try out different ways of arriving. So Cissy concentrates with all her might on the goal while remaining wholly spontaneous along the way, without a hint that she has the goal in her mind's eye. Cynthia never briefs us together; just as in our Film Board try-outs, the naturalness of a scene lies in the fact that we know nothing in advance except the objective. And Cissy is free to spring one-liners that make us laugh out loud.

Here are Cynthia and Sally in the house, their heads prayerfully bent. Cynthia's hands are clenched, her hair is pulled up and doubled back, so that a ponytail lies over the top of her head, a wisp of hair trails over her cheek. She and Sally are looking down at us with serious pre-scene faces as we sit at the makeshift table on which elements of our one and only film-breakfast are arranged: an orange, a croissant, a sandwich in plastic wrap. François is positioning a lamp, his hands held on either side of its head. Glimpses of direction held in planet-heads in photographs; while we eat, drink or wait, the directing heads are immobilized in anxious thought.

Cynthia wears jeans, a blue padded vest over a scarlet sweatshirt, or jumpsuits, white or Spanish-moss coloured. She wears black and white at parties; her hair free-falls over her shoulders. Her look in this photograph is simultaneously direct and faraway. Her head mills with questions—can she hang on to her vision of the finished film, the multiplicity of elements to be ordered? Though she may look like a Valkyrie, she is as ready to doubt herself as she is to break into one of her great laughs.

Out on the set, Cynthia and Sally lightly held the reins of authority. Inside herself, each was tensely concentrated, whereas Gloria, who had already done much of her day's work by writing the scenario, looked at times as though she didn't have a care in the world. Sometimes we heard Cynthia shout, "Glori-ah!!! Will you please come here?" Gloria, who had been hovering in my vicinity, jumped, then walked with nonchalant dignity down to the spot in the field where Cynthia, David, Roger and the cameras were almost hidden in the long grass. Cynthia and Gloria were inextricably linked together, as director and writer and old friends. Somehow they had succeeded in harmonizing their dreams for the film: Gloria's to have a strong lesbian presence; Cynthia's, to unlock the life hidden in old women. They were companions-at-arms, they engaged in behind-the-scenes shouting matches, punctuated by war cries: "Cyn-thee-*ahh!*" "Glor-ee-*ahh!*" to test each other's mettle. I witnessed one of these epic battles and was reminded of Tweedledum and Tweedledee, one with a saucepan, the other with a coal-scuttle on his head, wrapped in "bolsters, blankets, hearthrugs, tablecloths." "'Let's fight till six and then have dinner,' said Tweedledum." Like the twin brothers, Cynthia and Gloria were destined to explode in mutual exasperation and then make up and continue their amiable friendship.

Cynthia's mind stores up images rather than words. She perceives intuitively what bodies and faces are wordlessly saying. She makes a new film vocabulary out of the eloquence of old bodies, each of us defined by her shape, her distinctive way of labouring through long grass or up steps, of sitting, lying down, or dancing. We laugh, we generate our own laughter; our tears spring from memories of the past or fears for the future. With a minimum of coaching or coaxing, with only partial knowledge of our capabilities, Cynthia allows us to be, to develop our own action by the way we are. She takes risks. We are a kind of organic clay—or dough, self-rising? We don't need kneading. A semi-documentary is a happening within an artistic structure, which is set up with a delicate instinct for possibilities, for recognizing the moments at which possibilities happen.

Cynthia patiently waited for the central truth of each of us to appear and hold each of us steady from scene to scene as a gyroscope holds a ship steady. David de Volpi and Roger Martin provided a whole dictionary of images. Did any of us have a sense of being, in those thirty hours of film footage, material for misinterpretation? I remember thinking at one time, we have put ourselves in their hands; I remember feeling safe, sure that we would recognize and welcome our interpreted selves, translated into film-language. Cynthia kept her balance on a gleaming wire, high above obvious and less obvious dangers: sentimentality, flattery, and their converse—mockery. She was working with the tricky material of seven old women, outwardly pliable and inwardly vulnerable, each with her ego, her wish to be seen as—what? a best self? We, too, walked our tightropes, and at times lost and regained our balance in the process. Cynthia gave us the sense of being safe, and she and the others must, somewhere in the course of the filming, have begun to feel safe with us.

B I N D I N G

David de Volpi and Roger are making a glossary of images, an "interlinear translation," which situates us in a mysterious non-location between the lines. The real lines in Gloria's scenario, dated June 15, 1988, moved us along in time, placed us in a convincing fiction, made each of us into a character, often with an uncanny resemblance to the real person, to how each talked (Gloria's mind recorded our speech patterns), how each might react. She saw likelihoods: tempers, selfishness under stress, what each might be but would not always want to be. As it turns out, the interlinear translation enables us to speak a wishful language—how we want to be. Or so we think. We are, in fact, material for the camera, three-dimensional bodies who are being transformed into two-dimensional semi-fiction. A dimension is taken away from us and new ones are given as our molecules are bound with water, air, moonlight, sunlight, rain, to make something insubstantial—metaphors for old age and memory and death. We are bound, too, into metaphors for life: by birds, frogs, fish, mushrooms. We eat life, we make it when we laugh, dance, sing; we shout it ("We're alive!") and the hills send our words back to us. Do we think our words belong to us? Do we think any part of us belongs to us? It isn't so. Each word, each gesture is sustained by the cameras' insistence on contexts. The cameras must succeed in binding rickety old subjects into a landscape that will welcome us without irony; its beauty must become an extended image of us, a series of dream-images in which landscape is fused with seven old women. It provides water, the mother-image, the vessel for Constance's memories of childhood. Constance is joined to water, the hem of her dress touches it, she commits her old age to it when she drops her pills into the lake; it transforms her into memory's shimmering reflections. We call to her across water.

Every location (there were four) appears to have waited like the Sleeping Beauty to be found and waked by Cynthia, David, Sally and Gloria. I imagine their incredulous joy when, after passing through a big rain puddle (this, too, is a symbol), they get out of their van and climb the hill to the abandoned house they have seen from the road that seemed to lead nowhere. There is their metaphor: the house standing defiantly alone above the overgrown fields, the lake, woods and hills beyond. The crew will paint the interior of the house the colour of twilight; the house is both rickety and solid, it stands squarely on a concrete foundation. Pieces of it have fallen off, the porch sags. It echoes the extremities of old age. *Our* attitude when we arrive, moves from disdain to love: "Goodbye, house," Winnie says at the end. We bring the house to life as it brings us together; we come to love it, both on- and off-camera, because it brings us together.

The cameras see that the house is derelict and that we are derelict, lying in the dark with our shapes in sharp outline against the twilight-coloured walls, our anxious, sober or fearful faces illumined by light that has no source. The cameras are dispassionate, yet compassion, like the light without a source, also illumines us. It is the insubstantial matter of the film, an inaudible sonar, or echolocation. Connections, immediately obvious to the composite Them, between the house and us, are invisible to us until we see the film. We repudiate the house as we repudiate old age. "Old age is the pits," says Winnie in real life. "What a dump!" she says about the house when we enter it. But the house has its objective, the same as ours—to become one of the company of strangers. It begins to live to our rhythm, we give it life and bring life into it. We furnish it with found objects and with living grass to sleep on; it furnishes us with a dormitory, a dining room, a dance floor, and echoes the simplicity of our new state of being, which requires us to make something out of nothing. "I've got nothing," says Constance in the card game near the end of the film. "She laughs! She laughs!" says Michelle. The composite They know instantly that Constance's unexpected laughter in the old house is at the centre of a sonar signal that moves in concentric ripples to enclose the entire film.

Constance, who "sleeps a lot," as I say to Michelle, has dreamt the film. She is the dynamic source of connections, powered by the energy of a wish—to see her childhood house on the lake. The wish, more like a hypnotic command, steers the bus out of time and into the dream world of memory. Our escape routes are severed; the bus breaks down; Michelle sprains her ankle. "The bus will not move forward," says Gloria in her scenario. Michelle, our only young person, is now forcibly contained in a new medium—waiting—in which she cannot feel at home. Hobbled restlessness; she has to be in movement so she moves others. But these others, all of us except Catherine, are living in the vibrations of Constance's wish. Catherine and Michelle are both tuned to the outside world: Michelle is the first to hear when Catherine gets the bus started. Constance is asleep, and I am struck deaf, it seems, by not wanting to hear. Behind our apparent gloom when the bus breaks down again is our great reluctance to sever connections. Some of the happiest scenes in the film come after the final breakdown of the bus.

Catherine, whose action is movement, whose feet carry her away on a rescue mission, attempts to make a friend of the bus, whose action is immobility. She coaxes and cajoles it; she sings to it; when she kicks it she is kicking herself for her own failure. She realizes, finally, that the bus does not share her wish to get out, "to move forward," she takes over its original role as mover; her feet span the miles to rescue; she takes wing in the plane that reconnects all of us, only to return us to time and our separate lives in a final pulling-apart. Throughout the film there is a rhythmic swinging between motion (Catherine's walk out of the dream) and stasis (Constance asleep, a Sleeping Beauty like the house). And a binding, not only into the three elements—air, fire and water—but also to symbolic presences, inanimate beings that are extensions of ourselves. The old house on the lake, the boathouse on the lake, most of all, the rusty broken-down automobile, vintage—the time of our youth, down near the shed, in which Alice, Beth and Winnie sit to talk about a time long ago when they danced the nights away, fell in and out of love, lived the inebriating illusion of being alone on the dance floor with the chosen Him. And now they see these youthful selves when they look at young people in love, dancing together. There are criss-crossing connections woven with dazzling virtuosity in this scene. Alice, aged sixteen, is connected to the dance floor by a dangerously narrow path along the railroad bridge that spans the river between Kahnawake and Ville Lasalle. Alice, Beth and Winnie sit and remember in the old car, which has its own dashing past. Like a bridge themselves, they span the time between past and present. Their feelings are unchanged. Mr. Right might still come along. Little sexual sparks energize this scene, memories of the glorious feeling of falling in love. "Just talking about it makes me feel that I still could," says Beth with her flirtatious smile. The allegretto of youth, which has been dancing over a solemn adagio bass of age, drops down an octave; the theme is restated, andante, and the scene ends, as many sonatas do, with another adagio; still photographs of Alice, the child; Alice, the bride; Alice, mother and grandmother. Three ages of Alice. The fourth is here in the enclosing form of the old car as she remembers.

Mixing, not only in terms of sound, but also in the mixture of us: connection or binding, each with every other, and all of us with the elements. In the scenes in which we call to each other across water—Winnie to me, all of us to Constance, Catherine to all of us—we are mixed with symbols as well as with sound. We mix youth with age by going through the motions of youth; we are mixed by joining hands in a continuous turnover of partners on the dance floor, by splashing in the lake. Water, air, smoke, should be on the list of credits. Constance, who could not feel younger by going through the motions of youth, was bound to us, mixed with us, as a reminder, severe and sad, of our distance from youth.

Mixing in its largest sense included the composition of the film, with all its recognitions and identities. Live sounds, live music, live musicians, united their molecules with ours. Marie Bernard's chamber orchestra was invisibly there when Winnie, our dance-mistress and ballerina, danced to the music of Cimarosa. It is impossible to tell which echoes which, ourselves or the first half of the adagio phrase from Beethoven's trio, which climbs, hovers and breaks off, leaving the reflected descending image to be heard in imagination, like our future.

TEKAHAWÁKWEN

(A L I C E)

We are sitting eating chili con carne at the cardinal points of the
Montreal compass. Alice is north, Carla east, Pauline south, and
I'm west. Grandmother, daughter, granddaughter. Alice is
wearing one of her billowy creations, blue silk, mixed from pure
cobalt and pure cerulean; it is one of her majestic powers to give
the impression of being taller than she is; she does not need to
speak to be a commanding presence, from which her voice
sounds as deep voices sound in an immense high-vaulted chamber of a cavern. The instrument of her voice has tones and
half-tones, different timbres that can make a simple English
vocabulary extremely complicated; she uses the full range of it
in her own language, Mohawk; it is a great joy to me to hear
Alice speaking the music of her language. The fact that I don't
understand it brings its sound-patterns more directly into my
ears.

I set my tape recorder on the table and ask Alice to speak to me in Mohawk about her life. Pauline will translate into English.

Tekahawákwen (Alice): Ion'wesénhne shiiakwaksa'okón : 'a ne Kahnawake Iakwatatewennii : iohkwe tánon ion'wé:sen tsi iakwatkahri'tsherón : niskwe. Eniakwaterihwaienstá : na. Ehta' kéhshon nieniákwe. Entsákwawe ionkwaterihwaiensta'nonhne, sok nón:wa entsakwatawénha—akenhnhá : ke, "St. Lawrence River." Sewatié : rens ó : ni eniakwatenna'tsherénhawe "picnic" eniationniá : na. *Kahnekiióhstha (Pauline):* It was nice in Kahnawake when we were children. We were carefree, and we used to play so nicely. We'd walk to school. In summer we'd go swimming in the St. Lawrence River after school. Sometimes, we would take along some food and we'd have a picnic. I asked her, did they have chores to perform and she said most definitely, her chores were to debug the potato plants and her father was very strict and stern in that if he told his children to do it they had to do it or they couldn't go out and do what they wanted to do. Alice names the vegetables in Mohawk, some like carottes and cucumbers derived from French. She's talking about the vegetable garden and she's naming all the vegetables. The words she said are French words like "la carotte." Our words that we did not have in Mohawk are taken from the French, like my mother's father his first language was French after Mohawk. At that time their language was Mohawk, their mother tongue was Mohawk and then the first language they learned was French because . . . the missionaries were French-speaking. The farming communities close by were all French people, so our people, our Mohawk people, spoke French before they spoke English. At the turn of the century when they introduced schools to the reserve, we had nuns coming from Massachusetts—English-speaking nuns but a lot of the Massachusetts nuns, their parents were originally Québecois, and as a result they were bilingual nuns. They were called the Sisters of Saint Anne and they were a Massachusetts order. They came to live on the reserve; they had a convent. The majority of the people were all Catholics, so they ran all the schools for years and years and years but today we don't have any nuns left. At that time there was a large enough congregation that became Methodist or Protestant and then they had a separation; they had the children going to one school; of course, it was the Catholic school and then maybe twenty years ago they merged all the children in the village, and they just became like public schools so now all the children attend the same school. Except we have a school called the Indian Way School; they run their own school, their own curriculum; I think they even fund their own education and they teach what they want their students to learn, it's not controlled by the Department of Education or anything like that. They teach in Mohawk, they also teach in English but they also teach their own values. They push their culture. *Mary:* Alice, when you went to school, you were taught in English? *Pauline:* She said that when she went to school she went to school in English and at that time they had about a half hour of French a day and she never learned French in fact, she says she hasn't got a very high level of education; as a result she doesn't read and write that well. Her father used to travel around a lot in construction. He moved away many times from the reservation and each time he moved away he would take his family and they would have to leave school and go and live where the construction site was, so she was in and out of different schools and she didn't adapt very well. Alice says the place-names in English: Three Rivers, Niagara Falls, Wawa, Quebec, a lot of places, but then a lot of our men did move away during the wintertime to live in Lachine or Montreal. There were no bridges to cross at that time. The Mercier Bridge wasn't built, only the CPR bridge was there, and so they would have to walk the bridge. This was too treacherous in the cold of winter, so a lot of them moved with their families to the North Shore of the river during the winter months. But they would always come back. Six months or more would be the duration of the job depending on what they were building. They were working for Dominion Bridge Construction Co. in Lachine and this is why it took them into the outskirts to build. My grandfather, I think, went to school half a day, he didn't like it and he never went back to school but still he was able to become a boss on the job, he learned to read blueprints very well and he was self-taught for everything else and he did very well. My mother says he was admired because a lot of the people who were well educated had a lot of respect for him because of how he became self-taught. He worked on the bridge and he was also what you would call the pusher—the overseer, foreman. *Alice:* He worked at two bridges in Montreal. Victoria and Jacques Cartier. *Pauline:* He also worked at the Quebec bridge, the one that fell. He was working the time that the first bridge fell. Twice it fell and a lot of Indians were killed there—Fifty? sixty? were killed? *Carla:* You go in the cemetery and they're all lined up, there aren't that many of them. *Pauline:* But they didn't find all the bodies at the same time so as a result they're not all buried side by side. Some were found a long time later or after the disaster and probably some were buried with their family plots. [Alice speaks in Mohawk] *Pauline:* Oh, she says her father was working there both times the bridge collapsed. She was a little girl at that time. Well, it must have been the second time it fell, that you were there. You were born in 1914? *Alice:* Yeah. My father was working on that bridge. *Carla:* He wasn't actually on it when it fell. *Alice:* No, he just got home from lunch, so he used to go home for lunch and on the way coming back that's when it happened. *Pauline:* He was lucky.

Pauline: Well, you met this handsome man. *Alice:* I talk about it in the movie. *Mary:* In the photograph of him he's so handsome. *Alice:* Looks aren't everything, right? *Pauline:* She married at nineteen years old. She had known him about three years. He was from one end of town and she was from the other end of town. They call it the high and the low. A daughter was born to her in 1936 and her name was [she speaks in Mohawk] which would be my sister, her English name was Rachel. Shortly after she was born they moved to Detroit, Michigan, where my father was working. My mother always felt that the fact that she became pregnant while she was still nursing her first-born contributed to the first-born getting sick and dying. She said that the doctor had never realized that the child was sick, and she thinks the child became sick because she was pregnant and she was nursing. That could be an old wives' tale but she always had it in her head. She came to Kahnawake in '38; Rachel was born in '36, she came back in '38. When she went to Detroit she realized she was pregnant. I was born in '39. She never became well again—the child. Since the time she went to Detroit, she was sickly. No matter what she did she never regained her health and she lost her in March of 1939. *Alice:* March the third. *Pauline:* I was born a month after she died. So my mother always said she was never so happy because I was a girl because she had lost one and I replaced her. *Alice:* Today I'm still happy. [laughter] *Pauline:* She's still happy. Anyway . . . *Alice:* [to Pauline] These are our Indian names, our Mohawk names. *Pauline:* My sister's name was . . . I can't translate that because I don't know what it means. Kahnekiióhstha is my name and it means *One Purified the Water.* The *iostha* makes it good water. To drink or something like that, but that's my Indian name. And my daughter's name is Kawennakén:re. Mother's name is Tekahawákwen. I guess if you would shorten it you would say *Pathfinder.* Yes, *she picks up the path,* kind of. If you see somebody picking up the path, she can pick up the road take it with her. *Alice:* Kawennakén:re. *Pauline:* My youngest daughter's name is Kawennakén:re. We've lost a lot of our Mohawk language. For instance, if you say my youngest daughter's name, Kawennakén:re, to my ears it means someone who knocks things over. Kawennakén:re. My ancestors would know what that meant. This is my version of the name, anyway. *Carla:* We're more or less named after grandmothers who carry the same name, whereas we don't really pick them now, eh; I mean you can but you usually get named after your grandmother. *Pauline:* The names go down generation after generation. *Mary:* The English names don't have anything to do with the Mohawk names? *Pauline:* No, not at all. The Mohawk names are coming back into fashion, though for a while it was very seldom that anyone was called by their Mohawk name, everybody was using the English names, but now in the schools our little ones are going into Mohawk immersion and they're only called by their Mohawk names, and in fact, some people only give Mohawk names to their children. But then there has been a rebirth of culture and language, in the last ten, maybe fifteen years, to try and hold on to it to revive it. *Mary:* Every child learns Mohawk? *Pauline:* Well, no, not every child, it's still up to the parents. Some parents, in fact, will choose French over Mohawk because they feel that to earn a living they have to have the French language more than you need the Mohawk. *Carla:* [She tells a story of a child taught in Mohawk who was taken out because her parents thought she was lacking in other areas] In different subjects like the math. Sure she might be learning Mohawk but she was lacking in a lot of other things. *Pauline:* Because don't forget the only things we ever read were hymnals in Mohawk language, that's the only thing that the missionaries translated. I have copies of hymnals and prayer books in Mohawk but those were the only texts that were written. But as far as kindergarten and grade school subject matter, there's no available material. For instance, how do you teach math? There's no terminology of math in Mohawk you just can't, it's so . . . I don't know where to start. Mohawk is a beautiful language, it's very descriptive, it's just so different that it does take someone with a lot of patience to be capable of writing the curriculum in Mohawk for the schools. I think I was one of the last generations of people who grew up speaking Mohawk. In general, Mohawk was just about lost. You don't find too many people younger than I who are fluent. I was lucky, I spoke the Mohawk language because my father and

159

mother always spoke to me in Mohawk, as a child. I lived with my grandparents and neither of them could speak English; as a result, when I was a baby my mother had to work. My father and mother were separated when I was two years old. My father drank a lot and he abused my mother so at my age of two years old they finally separated. My mother says she always told my father that he was a ladies' man, drank, and did a lot of things to hurt her. She had a lot of patience but she always told him, "When my patience runs out it's gonna be finished. When we do separate, if you push me to that point, it's gonna be final. You'll never come back and say I'm sorry and then we'll start all over again, it'll be final, that's what will happen," and that's what happened. I was two years old. I don't remember my father at all, I remember glass breaking I can still hear glass breaking. My mother had a little restaurant and I remember coke bottles used to be in wooden crates at that time and the empties in the wooden crates would be piled up against the wall. I guess that's what fell over in one of their fights. I could hear all this glass breaking. I can still hear the glass breaking. Like I remember seeing my mother's leg cut and bleeding. Did you have a cut on your leg? *Alice:* [she speaks in Mohawk] and broken bottle cut. *Pauline:* And that I remember seeing blood on my mother's leg and I remember a blue coat, a child's blue coat and a blue hat—you know those bonnets that had those visors? A blue hat and I think it had blue velvet, and a coat and I remember wearing that coat and we were running, we were running away. And that's how I remember you know. My mother and I were running away. *Alice:* That was about four o'clock in the morning. *Pauline:* I'll never forget that blue coat because it just stayed in my mind and we were running through the fields or somewhere it seemed like fields. [Alice speaks in Mohawk] *Carla:* Was this the time that your marriage was over or it was just another fight? *Alice:* About a week after. This was about four o'clock in summer daylight. He [Alice's brother] saw my throat so he went through the field and he locked up

160

the door for your father to come out. He didn't come out. So, a few days after, I was out in this garden? *Pauline:* She had been taking the abuse for so long and . . . she said, well, that happened about a week before her final split with my father. She had been running in the field to her brother's house and she said it was just dawn becoming daylight when her brother answered the door and could see that she was all bruised on the neck and she said that she ran and he just, I guess, he was so angry by what he saw that he went to where my mother came out of our home, and he asked my father to come outside, but he didn't come out. So a few days later the same thing occurred with more trouble and that's when my mother decided to call it quits. She packed up all his belongings and she threw him out and that was it and she never saw him again and I never saw him again and I never heard from him, I never even got a card for Christmas, a five-cents card. *Alice:* I quit the restaurant because I didn't like the job, and took my work to distilleries where they make whiskeys. I didn't like the job, it's a sleepy job. [laughter] I worked there maybe, maybe not even a month. Then I fixed me a job at Dominion Rich, and then my sister Mary came back from Erie so we were talking what they pay. I think I used to get eighteen dollars a week. There's a lot of work up in Erie— she's got a good job so I made up my mind that I gotta go. I did good but [to Pauline] I left you behind. That's what hurts the most. *Pauline:* Did you get most of that? She had a sister in Pennsylvania who had a family there and came back and convinced her to work in the States where she'd do better. *Mary:* So that was during the war, wasn't it? *Alice:* Yeah. I worked in Erie where they make parts for airplanes. I used to . . . how do I explain? They used to call it a big hammer, and it comes down, part of the wing all different parts of the airplane. *Pauline:* They'd shape the aluminum. *Alice:* So I'll be standing there with a big can of oil and a mop and as soon as this hammer goes up then I have to oil it, the part that's going up, that was my job, eight hours a day. Each woman is standing where they keep this stocklist and I'm standing right there. I used to be sweating. *Pauline:* So my mother's used to hard work, she worked hard all her life but she said the worst part was leaving me behind when she went to the States because she had all the intentions of taking me, and my grandmother at the time convinced her not to take me because she said that her father's heart would be broken because we had been staying with my grandparents at that time when she moved away. Anyway, they encouraged her to leave me behind so my grandfather's heart wouldn't be broken because I was his pet. So this is why my background was full of Mohawk, because neither of them spoke English and this was the environment at Kahnawake hearing it all the time. Up to the time my grandmother died, she didn't speak English, not a word and neither of them were educated. My grandfather spoke a little English but he spoke French predominantly more than he spoke English, but his Mohawk language was his native language. [Carla reminds Alice to talk about work] *Alice:* Well, I worked in Erie, Pennsylvania '43 to '46. So I quit my . . . I didn't quit, I gave them leave of absence. I had to come home; my father's dying so I left in '46, I think. She was six years old, but I never went back. I stayed, so '47, I went and looked for a job in Lachine. *Pauline:* After she came back from the States she was called back from the States because my grandfather had taken sick, she asked for leave of absence. In the meantime he recovered so she was going to go back to her job that was waiting for her in Pennsylvania but my grandfather convinced her to stay and she realized that because I was at the age—I was six years old, you know, maybe she should stay, to devote herself to being a full-time mother, raise her child. So she found a job in Lachine and she stayed there thirty-three years until she retired. *Alice:* They used to make shoes and boots and slippers. I worked on everything. Whenever they need somebody, somebody's not in, they put me on that job and since I worked everything, every place I knew all the jobs there. This way I lost my finger. While I was there she got married. You got married at nineteen, hunh? *Pauline:* I was eighteen. *Alice:* Eighteen, and they had a big wedding for her. It was my vacation time when she got married, two weeks vacation. My helper that works with me, she goes to Detroit every time she gets a vacation because her family's there and that was the time she's getting married. So when she gets there her family took her out, they went to some bars, I guess, and she saw my husband. They went to this bar and she looked around—maybe my husband was there—she asked somebody they see him, they say, no, he just left here in fact, his glass is still standing there, so the friend said, don't worry, he'll be back. Well, she says, we were sitting there—her family—and we looked and he come back again, sat at the bar. So she said, "hello, guess who got married back home." "Well," he says, "I don't know." "Well," she says, "your daughter got married today it's her wedding day," so she said he just put his head down quiet and he got up and walked out. *Mary:* He's still alive? *Alice:* Oh yeah, he died about twenty years ago? Twenty-two years? *Pauline:* But I never got to meet him. *Alice:* He never came back. *Pauline:* And he died . . . we got a phone call one day and I think he died in a flophouse, something like that. So he was an alcoholic . . . *Alice:* He didn't like the way I used to treat him. I was married to him eight years. I couldn't change him. When he died I told her, "I'll give you your fare it's your father to go to the funeral." She didn't want. She said, "I don't know him, why should I go?" *Pauline:* I should be wasting my time to go and look at a stranger in a casket. It's a waste of money, a waste of time, we have nothing. Had we corresponded once in a while or even met but I never saw him. *Alice:* He never even sent a Christmas card. Those days you could buy a Christmas card for five cents and two-cent stamp. For her, for me I don't care never. *Pauline:* So she had a hard life. *Alice:* Ever since then I've been with them. They can't get rid of me. [laughter] The grandchildren are coming out they're all in their thirties. I'm still with them. Believe me I'm lucky to have a daughter that's got a roof over her head . . . . *Pauline:* Well, our home is your home. *Alice:* The house that my father left me it burned down. *Mary:* When was that? *Alice:* Oh, maybe about ten years now. *Carla:* Well, you never lived there, anyway. *Mary:* Carla, you have a sister. Are you all there together? *Alice:* Her daughter's in Ottawa. Here we have Louie [the chow]. *Pauline:* My mother thinks of Louie almost as a person. *Mary:* And where's Isaac? *Alice:* Oh, they've got their own home. They live on the reserve. That's Joe, the oldest one. We see them all every week; every Sunday my mother makes a traditional breakfast—they come for cornbread and steak every Sunday morning. So that's the routine; Isaac goes to pre-nursery school, Step by Step they call it. *Pauline:* That's so he'll have other kids around him. They're being taught in English, but like I say, it depends on parents what they want them to do, so I don't think they want him to go to total immersion. His mother's a nurse; she works on the reserve part time. *Alice:* So they all work, they go out in the morning and I'm left at home all day. *Mary:* You're at home all day? What do you do? *Alice:* Nothing. [laughter] I watch my programs. *Mary:* Aren't you lonely in the daytime in winter with the snow piled up? *Alice:* No. I know they're all coming back. I don't like to go out, the only time I go out is when they take me out. *Mary:* And then you go tooting off to Ottawa and Vancouver and Toronto. *Pauline:* She's certainly been travelling this year, a lot of mileage. *Mary:* The film was something wonderful, wasn't it? *Pauline:* We all had to coax her to take that acting job. She was very reluctant. And she complained every week, I mean, she'd complain and sort of back out and you know, it was our fault and she didn't feel like going back on Sunday. *Alice:* They're all swimming, they're having a barbecue or talking and I'd have to get ready to leave. *Carla:* Every week when she would come home, she always had stories to tell eh, she was always making us laugh. *Pauline:* I think that once she got there she didn't mind. It was the fact that you knew they were coming to get you in a little while and you had to go out again. Once she was actually there it wasn't too bad. *Carla:* And then when you had the break in the summer, she didn't want to go back, it was a long stretch. *Mary:* Did you find that the more it went on, the more fun it was? *Alice:* At the end, yes. *Pauline:* Well, we know that she made some good friends, she enjoyed that part. *Mary:* She's great in the film. *Carla:* She's herself, eh. I laughed so much because the expressions she comes out with—you can tell, that's my grandmother, it wasn't put on. *Alice:* I think everybody made a good person. *Mary:* Were you scared, Alice? Were you scared at the beginning? *Alice:* Yeah, I was nervous. *Mary:* Oh, me, too. It was awful. *Alice:* At first they started to tell us what to do. Then at the end . . . we did it our own way.

Pauline has sent me the English words for some Mohawk words:

karonhià:ke	sky
ó:kwire	tree
kaniataráhere	river, lake
atshennónnia	happiness
otsi'tén:'a	bird
karáhkwa	sun, moon
khe'kén:'a	my younger sister
Istén:'a	my mother
ontiatén:ro	my friend (masculine)
kheién:'a	my daughter
riién:'a	my son

ADAGIO
CON SPIRITO

"I'm here!" Constance cries in sudden anguish on the telephone. She has been talking about her past and I've listened without speaking. Disjointed phrases remain: "All my successes are in the past . . . I took the box and flung it out [her radio programs] . . . I didn't make a ripple in the world." "I want to die soon," she said, "I don't want to linger. Do you?" But we do want to linger, all of us; we have promises to keep (to ourselves), to linger without losing our marbles, as Constance once put it. At least a year ago she told me that she was losing her marbles; she had fallen into one of her temporary states of panic, could not find a word, or remember a friend's name. Sometimes she wakes up in a past that is more real to her than her present: "I was in my old house," she tells me, still terrified because her mind refused to take her back to her present apartment. One night she got out of bed in the middle of a nightmare, and, still asleep, woke up Denise, the young woman who takes patient care of her, who put Constance back to bed like a frightened child. "I didn't know where I was," says Constance.

"Time seems shorter for old people and longer for young people," I heard someone say on the radio. I can assure this person, who is probably young, that time for me can be as long or as short as it always was, but we do not necessarily move forward in it in the same old way, and memories appear with such startling clarity that they can displace what we see in front of our eyes. This is one of the perquisites of old age, I think, that memories can be viewed like film footage, that perhaps, after words and speech have gone, images will still flicker in our heads. As they do for Cissy, who is kept alive by the tube that feeds her, and sees one image—home, which has superseded all the others. "Can't I get out of here?" she asks Winnie, and her fingers lock on Winnie's arm with the full force of her will. "Take me home." She remembers the time in the hospital after her first stroke when she decided to get up and go home, forgets that her legs are useless and that she can no longer swallow. Her will, still alive, gives her a command that she is unable to obey: "Rise. Walk."

"You have to take life and chop it up and slice it down the middle and take what you get—awful things and now these nice things," says Beth on the telephone. Her life has been sliced up and recomposed like the magic apple in the film, which reappeared whole; Beth, glowing with happiness, looks herself like the apple. At 82, she is reborn, has become the actress of her dream. I see her on television, scarcely different from the winsome young woman we saw in her photographs, living proof of Cynthia's insistence: "You're *not* old!" Beth goes out on the town on CBC, plays video games, bowls for the first time and gets a strike on the second try. The bowling ball, a surrogate-Beth, wavers and wobbles a bit at first, and then, as if by

Beth's remote control, curves lazily, strikes, and ten pins fall in slow motion.

"Re Beth Webber." A telephone message has been left for Cynthia, and it materializes as one of the long lifelines the film has thrown out. I call Beth: "It wasn't some big cinema-man who'd seen something I'd done," she says. It was Eric, Tony, her son's best friend before Tony's death. Eric had seen a film clip of Beth taking off her wig, and had gone to see the film. Memories of Beth, his best friend's mother, spilled out to Cynthia and were passed on to Beth. Eric remembered how Beth lived in a semi-basement apartment, alone with Tony after her husband's death, how hard she worked, how "incredibly beautiful" she was. "He said I was incredibly beautiful," says Beth. "Somebody you haven't seen in twenty-five years!" Spin-offs that throw lines to the past. My first cousin's only child, Danny, whom I haven't seen for thirty years, calls from Toronto to recount the coincidence of seeing the film. "I recognized you," he says, "because you said wry things the way you used to. They just sort of slipped out."

"I'd give anything to hear it again," says Constance to me in the film. It saddens her not to be able to hear her favourite bird, the white-throated sparrow with its four-note song: a low introductory note and then three whistled notes, high and suppliant. "Oh, please, please, please," they seem to say. "Take me back to the time of happiness when I could hear that song," they say to Constance. "It goes like that," she says. She has whistled the song in a lower key with wonderful accuracy. Can she hear herself? She is 88 years old and her memory holds a birdsong, as real to her as the real one is to me. And what difference does it make that she can only hear the song that sounds in her memory; she has entered a state in which the outside world sounds more and more faintly but the world of memory takes possession of her. She and all of us are entering a realm where we will live more and more completely. Cissy has moved into this realm, taking with her regret and longing.

Perhaps she will let go of the fatal knowledge that still links her to the present, and will settle into the cozy, disordered space of her apartment and feel happy.

"We've put all that behind us," says Winnie about the film. She does not keep reviews; unlike Beth, who is amassing reviews, tapes, whatever reminds her of her dream come true, Winnie goes forward on her rounds, helping people, ending the day dead beat. But, in the film: "Still got our hopes . . . dreams," she said, sitting in the old jalopy with Alice and Beth. "It would be nice to meet somebody." Hopes, dreams, still stretching forward and memories stretching back. No, we haven't put it behind us, I think; it is living in us, it shows us how we were strangers and became company. We started with conspicuous differences and became company, almost without the use of words. "Don't use any long words," says Alice to me before our scene in which I cut the apple into seven pieces. I can hear her deep voice now, and remember the joy I felt at the thought: Alice knows me well enough to tease me. I remember little moments of confidence, how unease disappeared, was discarded. It was part of the unnecessary baggage that human beings carry around with them, part of a sense of difference. Out there we became friends, not out of difference but in harmony. "Dispersed are we, who have come together. Let us retain whatever made that harmony."

If we are being forced apart it is by death and illness and our own relentless aging. Gloria is dead but I am bound to her in the time when she was well, when she and Cynthia and Sally and all the others were drawn into our company and we into theirs. I find a photograph in which the crew are setting up the cameras with their legs straddled over rocks and moss. Gloria is standing in the background and her face is illuminated by the reflected light coming from a panel set up just above her head. She is looking meditatively out at the point where we are poised for a scene; she is wearing my plaid scarf, which I had ceremoniously wound around her neck when I shed my coat and hat to become a film-person.

Constance has just called and I tell her that I've been writing about her and the white-throated sparrow. She talks about the film. "All I can remember are sunny days. It never rained, did it?" I asked her, "Did you hear yourself whistling?" "Yes. I whistled the song of the white-throated sparrow. I could hear it."